OXFORD BOOKWORMS

ACTIVITY WORKSHEETS

STAGE 3

(1000 headwords)

OXFORD

UNIVERSITY PRESS

OXFORD
UNIVERSITY PRESS

Great Clarendon Street, Oxford OX2 6DP

Oxford University Press is a department of the University of Oxford.
It furthers the University's objective of excellence in research, scholarship,
and education by publishing worldwide in

Oxford New York

Auckland Cape Town Dar es Salaam Hong Kong Karachi
Kuala Lumpur Madrid Melbourne Mexico City Nairobi
New Delhi Shanghai Taipei Toronto

With offices in

Argentina Austria Brazil Chile Czech Republic France Greece
Guatemala Hungary Italy Japan Poland Portugal Singapore
South Korea Switzerland Thailand Turkey Ukraine Vietnam

OXFORD and OXFORD ENGLISH are registered trade marks of
Oxford University Press in the UK and in certain other countries

ISBN: 978 0 19 479088 8

Printed in Hong Kong

Illustrations by: Meshack Asare p 41; John Batten p 95; Rachel Birkett pp 116,
117; Jenny Brackley pp 124, 150; Sally Wern Comport/Shannon Associates pp
91, 92; Cory/Portland Studios, Greenville, USA pp 37, 39; Paul Dickinson pp 75,
76; Ramsay Gibb p 128; Neil Gower p 165; Simon Gurr pp 25, 26; Terry Hand
pp 54, 55; Nick Harris p 104; Paul Fisher Johnson pp 21, 23, 45, 47; Peterson
Kamwathi p 41; Chris Koelle/Portland Studios, Greenville, USA pp 29, 70, 71;
Fiona MacVicar pp 8, 11; Jan McCafferty p 160; Alan Marks p 109; Ian Miller
pp 33, 136, 137; Joseph Ntensibe p 41; Kwame Nyong'o p 41; Craig Phillips/
Shannon Associates pp 129, 132; Gareth Riddiford p112; Kate Simpson pp 156,
158; Adam Stower p 101; Techgraphics p19; John Tinniel p 144; Lynd Ward
courtesy of the Bodleian Library, Oxford (shelf mark 256 b 585) p 49; Adam
Willis/Artist Partners Ltd pp 66, 68

Cover illustrations (left to right) by: Paul Dickinson, Sally Wern Comport,
Alan Marks, Fiona MacVicar

*With thanks to all the Bookworms contributors who have written material for this book,
including:* Rowena Akinyemi, Jennifer Bassett, Helen Brooke, Steve Flinders,
Janet Hardy-Gould, Barbara Mackay, Alistair McCallum, Alan C. McLean, Julie
Reeves, Clare West

CONTENTS

INTRODUCTION

This book contains a set of photocopiable Activity Worksheets for each Stage 1 graded reader in the *Oxford Bookworms Library*.

Using Oxford Bookworms

Bookworms provide the extensive reading which all language learners need. Extensive reading allows students to extend their contact with English outside the classroom. This use of graded readers outside the classroom provides students with a wide range of language appropriate to their ability and interests; and their contact with the language takes place at their own speed – allowing assimilation of both structures and vocabulary. In addition, such reading generates a 'virtuous circle': provided the material they are reading is suitable for them, in terms of both grading and content, students begin to experience the pleasurable side of reading – and their desire to read increases. A small amount of classroom time (perhaps a few minutes a week) can generate several hours of reading, and many studies have shown that even a small amount of extensive reading has a powerful effect on students' learning and motivation.

Bookworms can be used in a whole-class project, or to provide more individualized reading. In a whole-class project, every member of the class reads the same book over the same period of time. This allows the teacher to provide a variety of support activities which can be carried out by the whole class. In individualized reading, teachers allow students to

read different books. Students are encouraged to choose readers on themes which interest them; but the teacher must be prepared to lose a little control over their reading. The *Bookworms Activity Worksheets* can be used with either of these approaches. In this way they provide a classroom focus for extensive reading outside the classroom.

Using Oxford Bookworms Activity Worksheets

Each Activity Worksheet includes up to four sections.

1 Introduction for the teacher (one page)

The **Introduction** is intended for the teacher. It contains a **summary of the reader's content**, intended to help teachers choose Bookworms which are appropriate to their classes. This summary may also help teachers to follow the stories of a number of Bookworms when students are involved in individualized reading. It should **never** be given to students, for two reasons. First, it gives the whole story or content, and thus removes the motivation for reading the text, and secondly, the language is not graded to the level of the Bookworms texts, and so will be far beyond the students' competence. Pre-reading texts for students are found in each Bookworm: the short 'blurb' on the back cover, and the introduction on the first page of the book. These are written to the same language level as the reader text, and are designed to arouse the students' interest without giving too much away. The Before

Reading Activities in the back of each Bookworm often check students' understanding of the Bookworms introduction and back cover 'blurb', and encourage imaginative speculation about the story and its characters.

The **Introduction** also usually contains a **Background** section. This may include information on the author. It will also include some information on the historical, social or geographical setting of the content. This is intended to help teachers set the context for students' reading and arouse their interest in finding out more by reading.

Finally, the **Introduction** usually includes a **Before Reading** section. This provides suggestions for encouraging interest among the students before they begin reading, and includes suggestions on using cover image, back cover blurb, story introduction, and audio recording.

2 Pre-reading activities (one page)

These are photocopiable activities which students should carry out individually, or in groups, before they start reading.

In many cases, these activities will encourage students' interest in the theme of the Bookworm. In addition, they may provide some language input – of vocabulary, for example – which will help students when they start reading.

In many cases, these activities will be open-ended – generating discussion and reflection. There may not always be a 'correct' answer.

Detailed instructions **To the teacher** (including, where appropriate, an answer key) are included at the bottom of the page. **These should not be copied for students.**

3 While reading activities (up to three pages)

These photocopiable activities are intended to help consolidate the students' reading, ensuring that they have understood a section of the story, and perhaps encouraging them to speculate on what will happen next. This anticipation of what will come on the next page, or in the next chapter, is an important part of the reading process – the student needs to have a hypothesis of where the story is going, with which to compare what is actually being read.

In most cases, these activities should be used at specific points in the story – the precise point will be indicated in the **To the teacher** section. Again, these activities may be suitable for individual or group work and they may be open-ended.

Detailed instructions **To the teacher** (including, where appropriate, an answer key) are included. These should not be copied for students.

4 After reading activities (up to three pages)

The photocopiable activities in this section build on the experience of reading. They are not tests, although in most cases they will require a good understanding of the text. Frequently, considerable reading or re-reading may be required. (To test reading, teachers should make use of the photocopiable tests provided for each level in the *Oxford Bookworms Library Tests*.)

Detailed instructions **To the teacher** (including, where appropriate, an answer key) are included. **These should not be copied for students.**

The activities in this book can be complemented by activities created by the teacher, or, better still, by students for other students. An excellent After reading activity is for a student (or group of students) to create a Pre-reading activity for students who have not yet read a particular Bookworm.

Using Oxford Bookworms Audio

Audio recordings are now available for a wide range of Bookworms. Each recording contains the full text of the book, read naturally by professional actors, but with the speed carefully controlled so that students' comprehension is not too heavily challenged.

Recordings can be used as an introduction to a book, or as a way of encouraging reading once students are already part of the way through a book. Many students like to listen to recordings without looking at the accompanying book, in their free time.

As the Inspector Said and Other Stories

Retold by John Escott

Introduction

The stories

As The Inspector Said. Sonia French is bored with her husband Robert who is more interested in his collection of silver than in her. She and her lover Charles Darrell devise a plan to murder Robert. But the plan goes wrong and it is Charles who ends up dead.

The Man Who Cut Off My Hair. Judith can lip-read and sees two men talking on the train about some silver in the cottage of a man she knows. Passing the cottage later, she sees the same men inside. They tie her up and cut off her hair which makes her furious. She keeps on their trail by reading their lips twice more until finally the gang is arrested and the silver recovered.

The Railway Crossing. Dunstan Thwaite decides to murder John Dunn because he is blackmailing him. But part of Dunstan's plan goes wrong and he decides not to commit the act. Ironically, Dunn dies anyway; all the evidence points to Dunstan as the murderer; and he goes to his death for a crime which, technically, he did not commit.

The Blue Cross. Valentin, the chief of the Paris police, is in London trying to catch Flambeau, the international criminal. Flambeau disguises himself as a priest because he wants to steal a valuable blue cross from Father Brown. But Father Brown guesses his intention and outwits him by leaving a trail of clues for the police to follow.

Cash on Delivery. Max Linster is a professional killer, hired by Jacob Elliston to murder his wife. He hides in the wife's room but her servant comes in and he strangles her instead. Not realising the mistake, Elliston pays him cash on delivery – of the body.

Background to the stories

As the text on the back cover tells us, these stories are all taken 'from the golden age of crime writing'. Not all the writers are well-known. However, Cyril Hare (real name A. A. Gordon Clark, 1900–58) was a lawyer as well as a writer; Freeman Wills Crofts (1879–1957) was an Irish railway engineer who often used his knowledge of railways in his stories; and G.K. Chesterton (1874–1936) was one of the outstanding writers and essayists of his day: his Father Brown, about whom he wrote stories from 1911 to 1927, is one of the great fictional detectives of the century. (There is a collection of Father Brown stories in the Oxford Progressive English Reader series, although at a rather higher level than this volume.)

There are a number of other crime stories available in the Oxford Bookworm Series at each level (see the Oxford Graded Reader catalogue) and you might like to encourage your class to make comparisons between them and to develop their reading ability through looking at several different examples of this type of story; and even to do a project on the historical development of crime fiction from its origins to the present day.

Before reading

Here are some ways to help your students approach the story:

1   Give students the title of the book and show them the picture on the cover. Ask them to try and guess what kind of the story it is.

2   Give students a copy of the text on the back cover of the book, and of the story introduction on the first page. When they have read the texts, ask them a few questions about the story, or use the Before Reading Activities in the back of each Bookworm.

3   Use the pre-reading activity in this worksheet.

4   If there is a recording of this title, play the first few pages and stop at an interesting point.

As the Inspector Said and Other Stories

Pre-reading activity 1

Match the pictures to the stories

a 'That child is watching us.'

b 'The place with the broken window!'

c 'It's sensible to be careful.'

d Next he put a hammer into one-pocket of his overcoat, and a torch into the other-pocket.

e 'The money is safe in my bedroom.'

f 'A hundred pounds,' he said again.

g 'If you don't believe me, feel this.'

h He was careful to clean the small gun that was in his dressing-gown pocket.

i 'If you're the police and you've come about that parcel, I've-already sent it off.'

j The man with the blue eyes moved towards me with the knife.

To the teacher

Aim: To familiarize students with the setting

Time: 10–20 minutes

Organization: Give one copy of the worksheet to each student or to each pair of students. Ask the students to match each picture with a caption. Then, tell them the titles of the stories and ask them to match two pictures to each title. When they have finished this, ask them to imagine what each story could be about. Students need only make intelligent guesses about the stories from the information they already have.

Key: 1h, 2f, 3e, 4b, 5g, 6j, 7c, 8i, 9a, 10d.

As the Inspector Said and Other Stories

Pre-reading activity 2

Word search

A	L	A	R	M	B	E	L	L	W
B	T	L	T	C	L	U	E	D	H
U	T	I	E	D	A	N	J	I	I
R	O	B	I	S	C	J	E	V	S
G	R	I	R	T	K	M	W	O	K
L	C	H	H	A	M	M	E	R	Y
A	H	F	K	I	A	G	L	C	O
R	O	P	E	N	I	Z	S	E	Z
Y	R	K	G	U	L	B	H	F	T
W	H	I	S	P	E	R	Y	K	D

DEFINITIONS:

1 a bell to warn someone of danger
2 something to show you were not there when the crime happened
3 getting money from someone by saying you will tell bad things about them
4 when someone has broken into a house to steal
5 some thing or piece of information that helps to find the answer to a mystery or crime
6 to finish a marriage by law
7 something which is used to hit things when fixing them together

8 rings, etc with valuable stones in them
9 something used to tie up something or somebody
10 a dirty place on something
11 to put a piece of rope round someone or something
12 a small light which is carried to show the way in the dark
13 a strong drink
14 to speak very quietly

To the teacher

Aim: To introduce key vocabulary
Time: 10–15 minutes
Organization: Give out the worksheet and ask students alone or in pairs to find as many words as possible in five minutes. Then ask them to match the words they have found with the following definitions (adapted from the glossary at the back of the book).

Go through the words and deal with any remaining difficulties over meanings. Finally ask students what kinds of story might include these words.
Key: alarm bell, alibi, blackmail, burglary, clue, divorce, hammer, jewels, rope, stain, tied, torch, whisky, whisper.

As the Inspector Said and Other Stories

After reading activity 1

A–Z Ordering puzzle

Re-order these sentences from **The Man Who Cut Off My Hair.**

	SENTENCE	ORDER
a	I was more angry than I thought possible.	
b	Then a man got in and sat beside the one who was already there.	
c	We got to Victoria Station and went to the cloakroom.	
d	I followed him up the stairs.	
e	The man with the blue eyes moved towards me with a knife.	
f	'Cotterill, Cloakroom, Victoria Station, Brighton Railway.'	
g	They both got out at the station before our village.	
h	The man with blue eyes put his lips near to the other man's ear.	
i	What I saw surprised me very much.	
j	It took many years for my hair to grow long again, and it never grew as long as before.	
k	Jewels!	
l	He had fair hair and blue eyes.	
m	I teach people who are deaf and dumb, and I teach them by lip-reading.	*1*
n	I did not sleep that night.	
o	The police caught all the thieves.	
p	My walk took me past Myrtle Cottage.	
q	I saw a man carrying a parcel, and I saw the man who was going to speak to him.	
r	My head felt strange.	
s	I was thirteen years old when it happened.	
t	And we went in, the detective first and me behind him.	
u	But we got the parcel.	
v	The shop at number 13 sold jewels and less valuable things.	
w	He was not a young man, but he climbed in through that window as quickly as a boy.	
x	There were several men in there, but I was only interested in one.	
y	At first they thought I was crazy.	
z	'Judith is an excellent lip-reader,' said Mr Colgate.	

To the teacher

Aim: To order, revise, remember what has been read, to summarize (The Man Who Cut Off My Hair)
Time: 10–20 minutes
Organization: Give out the worksheet to pairs or groups of students. Once students have put the sentences from the story in the right order, they can also use them to retell the story in their own words.
Key: a9, b3, c16, d23, e8, f11, g5, h10, i7, j26, k19, l4, m1, n12, o25, p6, q17, r14, s2, t22, u18, v21, w13, x24, y15, z20.

As the Inspector Said and Other Stories

After reading activity 2

Five years later

For each character discuss what happened five years after the story. Choose from the three statements or add your own.

Robert French (in *As the Inspector Said . . .*)

1 Sonia died in a mysterious car accident and Robert lived alone with his silver.
2 Sonia found Robert's gun and he went to prison for murder.
3 He became angry because Sonia got a new friend. But he had a plan . . .
4 Your own idea.

The man with blue eyes (in *The Man Who Cut Off My Hair*)

1 He came out of prison and tried to cut Judith's throat.
2 He fell in love with Judith but she would not marry him because he had cut off her hair.
3 He learnt to lip-read and began to teach deaf and dumb people in prison.
4 Your own idea.

Hilda Thwaite (in *The Railway Crossing*)

1 She left the country when people began to say that she was the wife of a murderer.
2 She was happy to stay in the same house after the death of her husband.
3 She was very unhappy and had to go away because she had no more money.
4 Your own idea.

Flambeau (in *The Blue Cross*)

1 He escaped from prison and became an international criminal once more.
2 Father Brown visited him every week in prison and they became friends.
3 Flambeau died in prison.
4 Your own idea.

Jacob Elliston (in *Cash on Delivery*)

1 He was very unhappy after Linster's visit and shot himself.
2 He went to prison for the murder of Josephine Demessieux.
3 He lived happily with his wife.
4 Your own idea.

To the teacher

Aim: To revise and interpret characters (all stories)
Time: 10–15 minutes
Organization: Give out the worksheet and ask each pair of students to discuss what happened to the characters five years after the end of the relevant story. After time for discussion, pairs should report back to the whole class so that the whole class deals with each character in turn.

Australia and New Zealand

Christine Lindop

Introduction

Chapter summary

Chapter 1 (An enormous land) looks at key facts about the geography, climate, and population of Australia. The country is the fifth biggest in the world but has a population of only 20 million. Around two-thirds of Australia is desert so most people live in cities close to the coast.

Chapter 2 (Australia's past) explains that the first people in the country were the Aborigines who arrived over 40,000 years ago. However, Captain James Cook claimed Australia for Britain in 1770, and in 1787 the British started to send convicts there to build roads and farms. In 1901 the six separate Australian states became one country.

Chapter 3 (Eight cities and the outback) introduces the Australian cities of Sydney, Melbourne, Brisbane, Adelaide, Perth, Hobart, Darwin, and the capital Canberra. Canberra is the newest Australian city and is located in its own territory rather than a state. The outback is the flat, hot centre of Australia.

Chapter 4 (The Aborigines) describes how the Aborigines had originally lived a nomadic lifestyle, living off wild plants and animals. However, when the British arrived they started to take much of their land and the Aboriginal population started to decline. Today, the population has increased again and they have claimed back some of their land.

Chapter 5 (Uluru and other wonders) looks at some of the amazing places to visit in Australia such as Uluru, an enormous rock in the desert which is over 600 million years old, and the Great Barrier Reef, the world's longest coral reef.

Chapter 6 (Sheep, cattle, minerals and wheat) shows that Australia is a rich country and much of its money has come from sheep, cattle, minerals, wheat, and wine.

Chapter 7 (A faraway land) introduces New Zealand – a long, narrow country with two main islands: the North Island and the South Island. The population is only 4.1 million people.

Chapter 8 (New Zealand's past) describes how nobody lived in the country until the Maōri people arrived a thousand years ago. In 1642 the Dutch sailor Abel Tasman came to the islands and gave New Zealand its name. Captain James Cook visited the country four times between 1769 and 1777 and in 1840 Captain William Hobson wrote the Treaty of Waitangi claiming the country as British.

Chapter 9 (Five cities) describes New Zealand's major cities: Auckland, the capital Wellington, Christchurch, Dunedin, and Hamilton.

Chapter 10 (Maōri) explains about the original Maōri population of New Zealand. When the British came Maōri lost a lot of their land and their population dwindled. In the twentieth century many aspects of Maori language and culture saw a revival and they regained some of their land. However, some Māori still experience health and social difficulties.

Chapter 11 (Wonders of New Zealand) describes the wonders of New Zealand which include the volcanoes around the city of Auckland and the Fox Glacier on the South Island.

Chapter 12 (Ten sheep and two cows) shows that although only one in ten New Zealanders work on a farm nowadays, agriculture is still highly important.

Chapter 13 (Free time and sport) looks at sport in both Australia and New Zealand. Water sports such as swimming and sailing are important, and there are also four different types of football.

Chapter 14 (Animals, birds, and plants) describes the unusual wildlife in the two countries.

Chapter 15 (Famous people) looks at famous Australians including the runner Cathy Freeman and the film star Russell Crowe. Famous New Zealanders are the climber Sir Edmund Hillary and the rugby player Jonah Lomu.

Chapter 16 (Today and tomorrow) considers the changing face of the two countries which are now developing stronger relationships with other nations in the Pacific.

Australia and New Zealand

Pre-reading activity

Word search

Look at the definitions and find the words in the word search below.

V	O	L	C	A	N	O	W	G	O	L	D	K
Z	K	D	A	E	K	W	I	R	S	X	C	A
G	Y	E	T	M	O	F	N	Q	H	U	O	N
E	L	S	T	I	A	V	E	K	E	M	N	G
Y	Q	E	L	G	L	A	C	I	E	R	V	A
S	X	R	E	Z	A	D	V	B	P	F	I	R
E	W	T	J	X	M	K	I	W	I	Y	C	O
R	B	C	O	R	A	L	R	E	E	F	T	O
M	E	A	R	T	H	Q	U	A	K	E	B	Q

DEFINITIONS:

1   a person who has been sent to prison for doing something wrong
2   a long line of rocks in the sea that are made from the bones of very small animals
3   a large, dry area of land with very few plants
4   a sudden strong shaking of the ground; buildings sometimes fall down when this happens
5   a mountain with a hole in the top where fire and gas sometimes come out
6   animals that people keep on farms for their meat and wool
7   cows and bulls that people keep on farms for their meat
8   an alcoholic drink made from grapes
9   a yellow metal that is worth a lot of money
10   a river of ice that moves slowly down a mountain
11   a place where hot water or steam suddenly come up into the air from the ground
12   a big wild animal that jumps on its strong back legs
13   a wild animal, like a small bear, that lives in eucalyptus trees and eats the leaves
14   a small wild bird that lives on the ground and cannot fly

To the teacher

Aim: To introduce key vocabulary and encourage students to predict information about Australia and New Zealand
Time: 40–45 minutes
Organization: Give one copy of the worksheet to each group of students. Tell the students that they have ten minutes to find as many words as possible. Then ask them to match the words they have found with the definitions (some of which are taken from the glossary). Go through the words and deal with any remaining difficulties over meanings.
Then ask the students to sort the words into three groups: Australia, New Zealand or both countries. Answers are below

for teacher reference. Don't tell students whether they are correct in their predictions. Ask them to look back later at this activity to see if their ideas were right.
Key 1: convict, 2 coral reef, 3 desert, 4 earthquake, 5 volcano, 6 sheep, 7 cattle, 8 wine, 9 gold, 10 glacier, 11 geyser, 12 kangaroo, 13 koala, 14 kiwi.
Australia: convict, coral reef, desert, kangaroo, koala. New Zealand: earthquake (there tend to be more in New Zealand than Australia), volcano (active volcanoes are rare in Australia), glacier, kiwi, geyser. Australia and New Zealand: sheep, cattle, wine, gold.

Australia and New Zealand
While reading activity

The history of the two countries

Put the following events in the correct order.

	Australia – events	order		New Zealand – events	order
a	Britain started to send convicts to Australia		a	Captain James Cook visited the islands four times	
b	The six different Australian states became one country		b	Women got the vote for the first time	
c	Gold was found in New South Wales and Victoria		c	Māori people came from islands in the Pacific Ocean to live in the country	
d	Captain James Cook landed and said that Australia belonged to Britain		d	Soldiers from New Zealand fought in the first and second world war	
e	The first National Sorry Day was held to say sorry for Aboriginal children who were taken from their parents		e	Five women had the most important jobs in the country	
f	Aborigines came from South East Asia to live in the country		f	Captain William Hobson wrote the Treaty of Waitangi and 40 Māori chiefs agreed to it	
g	Sydney Opera House was opened		g	New Zealand became a nuclear-free zone	
h	Dutch sailors Willem Janszoon and Abel Tasman visited the country		h	Gold was found in the South Island	

To the teacher

Where: At the end of chapter 8

Aim: To revise key information about the history of the two countries

Time: 30–40 minutes

Organization: Ask students about the first people to live in Australia and New Zealand. Tell students they are going to look at key events in the history of both countries. What other things can they remember about the history of the two nations? Give out the worksheets to small groups of students. As a class identify the first historical event for each country (Australia – f, New Zealand c). Then in groups

encourage them to discuss which events will come earlier or later for each country. Students then write in pencil the order of the events. Finally, students check with chapter 2 and chapter 8 of the book, where most of the information comes from. Conduct feedback as a class. Encourage students to say more information about each event e.g. What was special about women getting the vote in New Zealand? – They were the first women in the world to have the vote.

Key 1: Australia: a 4, b 6, c 5, d 3, e 8, f 1, g 7, h 2. New Zealand: a 2, b 5, c 1, d 6, e 8, f 3, g 7, h 4.

Australia and New Zealand
After reading activity

A factfile for tourists

Complete the factfiles about Australia and New Zealand.

Australia

Capital city:

Interesting cities to visit:

Special places to visit:

Birds, animals and trees to see:

Sports to watch:

Sports to do:

Things to eat:

New Zealand

Capital city:

Interesting cities to visit:

Special places to visit:

Birds, animals and trees to see:

Sports to watch:

Sports to do:

Things to eat:

To the teacher

Aim: To revise the key features of the two countries
Time: 40–50 minutes
Organization: Tell students they are going to write a factfile about Australia and New Zealand for tourists who want to visit the country. Give each pair of students a copy of the worksheet. Elicit as a class the type of thing they could write in each category. Students look back at the book and write their ideas on a piece of rough paper. Monitor and help students with any problems. Students then complete the photocopied factfiles.
Key: Possible answers: Australia: population – 20 million,

capital – Canberra, interesting cities - Sydney and Melbourne, special places – Uluru and the Great Barrier Reef, birds, animals and trees – emus, koalas and eucalyptus trees, sports to watch – horse racing, sports to do – Australian rules football, things to eat – kangaroo meat.
New Zealand: population – 4.1 million, capital – Wellington, interesting cities – Auckland and Christchurch, special places – Fox Glacier and Hot Water Beach, birds, animals and trees –
kiwis, tuataras and kauri trees, sports to watch – rugby, sports to do – sailing, things to eat – food cooked in hangi style.

The Brontë Story

Tim Vicary

Introduction

The story

The story opens in 1855, and Patrick Brontë, the rector of Haworth, tells the story of his family. He, his wife and their six children – Maria, Elizabeth, Charlotte, Branwell (their only son), Emily and Anne – moved to Haworth in 1820 but his wife died in 1821 and her sister, Aunt Branwell, came to look after the children in her place.

In 1824, Patrick sent four of the children away to Cowan Bridge School but the two eldest fell ill and died, and he brought the two others home again. The children stayed at home and played together, writing stories in little books.

Later, Charlotte and Anne went to another school but Anne fell ill and they came home again. Branwell's move to London to train as an artist was short-lived and he too returned.

In order to earn money, the sisters decided to start their own school. Charlotte and Emily moved to Brussels to improve their French.

Then Aunt Branwell died and Emily returned to look after the family. Charlotte returned a year later but their school was a failure. Branwell was in love with the mother of the children being taught by Anne and his mental state was seriously affected after being forbidden to see her.

By 1845, Branwell was drinking heavily but the three sisters had a book of their poems published, Patrick had a painful eye operation, and in 1847, Charlotte had *Jane Eyre* published under the pseudonym Currer Bell.

Soon after, Anne's *Agnes Gray* and Emily's *Wuthering Heights* also appeared but in 1848 both Branwell and Emily died.

Anne died a year later but Charlotte's reputation grew. In 1854, Charlotte married Patrick's curate, Arthur Nicholls but she died during pregnancy in 1855.

Background to the story

The Brontë Story provides us with valuable information about the Brontë sisters but is also a gripping but tragic story in its own right. The Brontë family is a unique grouping in the history of literature and this book uses the device of having the father narrate its story, to give us an insight into the circumstances which fostered the talents of the three writers who between them produced some of the greatest novels in the English language. We see how the genius of Charlotte, Emily and Anne developed as a result of their own individual experiences and yet needed the presence of the others to flourish; and we are given a vivid portrait of the wild, hard and austere Yorkshire countryside which is such an important element in their books. We learn something of the individual characters of the three; and of the malign influence of their brother Branwell – the dreadful inspiration for Arthur Huntingdon in Anne's *The Tenant of Wildfell Hall*. We are also confronted with the remorseless nature of the family's tragedy as mother, aunt and children all die in turn – not one of the Brontë children reached the age of forty.

Before reading

Here are some ways to help your students approach the story:

1 Give students the title of the book and show them the picture on the cover. Ask them to try and guess what kind of the story it is.

2 Give students a copy of the text on the back cover of the book, and of the story introduction on the first page. When they have read the texts, ask them a few questions about the story, or use the Before Reading Activities in the back of each Bookworm.

3 Use the pre-reading activity in this worksheet.

4 If there is a recording of this title, play the first few pages and stop at an interesting point.

The Brontë Story
Pre-reading story

Chapter titles

Match the chapter titles with the sentences.

1 Haworth

2 Cowan Bridge School

3 The little books

4 Growing up

5 Looking for work

6 Monsieur Héger and Mrs Robinson

7 Currer, Ellis, and Acton Bell

8 The best days, and the worst days

9 Arthur Nicholls

a 'Papa', she said. 'We want to start a school.'

b When he stopped coughing, it was because he had stopped breathing.

c The next day they invented another story, and then another.

d 'Yes, papa. It's a man's name, with the same first letters: . . .

e My name is Patrick Brontë and I am seventy-eight years old.

f '. . . your daughter Charlotte and I would like to be married.'

g I wanted my children to go to the best school I could find.

h So Charlotte went back to Brussels alone.

i Charlotte went to school again when she was fifteen.

To the teacher

Aim: To familiarize students with the setting
Time: 10 minutes
Organization: Give one copy of the worksheet to each student or to each pair of students. Ask the students to match chapter titles with sentences from the book. The chapter titles are in order.

When they have completed the exercise, ask them: From what you have seen and read so far, what do you think *The Brontë Story* is about and who are the main characters?
Key: 1e, 2g, 3c, 4i, 5a, 6h, 7d, 8b, 9f.

The Brontë Story

While reading activity

Whatever next?

Writes a book and becomes rich and famous	Becomes an important man in the Church
Lives longer than all his children	**PATRICK**
Stays in the same house in Haworth until the end of his life	Something else

Dies before he is forty	Falls in love with the mother of the children to whom Anne is governess
BRANWELL	Something else
Goes to London and becomes a famous painter	Loses the woman he loves and starts to drink a lot

Falls in love with a man who is already married to another woman

Dies when she is expecting a baby

CHARLOTTE

Gets married to the man who helps her father in the church in Haworth

Something else

Writes books which people still read today and becomes famous

Falls in love with a man who goes mad	Spends a lot of time walking in the wild Yorkshire countryside
Something else	**EMILY**
Writes a successful book called *Wuthering Heights*	Becomes famous and goes to London a lot

Becomes a governess in a big house	Something else
ANNE	Looks after her father until he dies
Dies one year after her return from Roe Head	Writes a book called *The Tenant of Wildfell Hall*

To the teacher

Where: At the end of Chapter 4

Aim: To analyse the story closely, based on partial reading of text

Time: 15–30 minutes

Organization: Divide the students into groups and give them the worksheet or show it on an overhead projector. Ask students to consider the several possibilities of what could happen to some of the key people in the book, giving reasons for their choices of outcome. Tell them that, for each person, the options presented could all be right, could all be wrong or could be a mixture of right and wrong. You can record their decisions and then return to them again when they have finished the whole book.

The Brontë Story

After reading activity

Dates and places

Match each date with the correct description(a–l).

1820	a	Patrick's eldest children, Maria and Elizabeth, both died.
1821	b	Branwell went to London to learn to be an artist.
1824	c	Jane Eyre and Wuthering Heights were published.
1825	d	Arthur Nicholls moved to Haworth.
1835	e	The Brontë family moved to Haworth.
1842	f	Charlotte and Emily went to Monsieur Héger's school in Brussels.
1845	g	Anne died.
1847	h	Patrick sent four of his children to school at Cowan Bridge.
1848	i	Charlotte died.
1849	j	Patrick's wife, Maria, died.
1854	k	Charlotte married.
1855	l	Branwell and Emily died.

Match the sentences (a–j) with the places on the map (1–10)

4 a Aunt Branwell came from here.

☐ b Charlotte and Emily went to school here.

☐ c Branwell went here to become a painter and Charlotte to meet famous writers.

☐ d Charlotte took Patrick here to see an eye doctor.

☐ e Patrick Brontë went to university here.

☐ f Anne died here.

☐ g The Brontë family moved here.

☐ h Patrick Brontë and Arthur Nicholls both came-from here.

☐ i Charlotte and Arthur had a holiday here after-they married.

☐ j Patrick paid for Branwell to have a room here.

To the teacher

Aim: To revise events in the book through the perspectives of chronological development and of geography

Time: 20 minutes

Organization: Students can work alone or in pairs to match the events in the book (a–l) with the dates 1–12. They should do this without the book although they might check when they complete the exercise. When they have done this, ask students to match the sentences with the places on the map.

Key 1: e, j, h, a, b, f, d, c, l, g, k, i.

Key 2: 1h, 2e, 3g, 4a, 5c, 6j, 7b, 8d, 9f, 10i.

The Call of the Wild

Jack London

Introduction

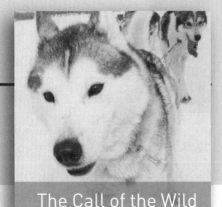

The Call of the Wild

JACK LONDON

The story

Buck is a large dog, living in a comfortable home in California in 1897. In the Yukon it is the time of the great Gold Rush, and Buck is kidnapped and taken north to Canada to be sold – for three hundred dollars— as a sledge dog.

His first owners, who buy him in Skagway, Alaska, are François and Perrault, who carry letters and official papers for the postal service. Buck quickly learns the work of a sledge-dog and after a fight in which he kills the lead-dog Spitz, Buck becomes lead-dog on the sledge. Buck pulls the sledge to Dawson City in the Yukon and back with François and Perrault, and then makes the trip again with two other men. He works hard but he is well-treated by the sledge drivers.

After the second journey to Dawson City and back Buck is bought by two Americans, Hal and Charles who are travelling north together with Mercedes – Hal's sister and Charles's wife. They are new to the North and have no idea how to drive a sledge or look after dogs. Most of the dogs die on the journey and in the end the sledge itself disappears through the ice on a frozen river and only Buck survives – saved by John Thornton.

John looks after Buck (who is tired, thin and ill), and the man and the dog become the best of friends. Later in the year Buck saves Thornton's life when he falls into a river and in the winter Thornton and his partners Hans and Pete win fourteen hundred dollars betting that Buck can pull a sledge carrying three hundred and fifty kilos.

The three men travel east with their dog team, looking for gold, which they find in the bed of a lake. But Buck, despite his love for Thornton, is being increasingly attracted to the wild forests – and to the wolves that live there. He disappears for long periods, and one day he returns to the camp to find that it has been attacked by Yeehat Indians, and all the dogs and the men are dead. He attacks, and drives away the Yeehats. There is nothing, now, to stop Buck returning to the wild. He joins a pack of wolves and lives the rest of his life following the call of the wild.

Background to the story

The story is set against the background of the Yukon Gold Rush when thousands of people flooded to the north-east of Canada to hunt for gold. The journey to the goldfields taken by Buck from Skagway was that taken by most of the gold hunters and it was a truly terrible journey on which many died. The first part of the journey, up the Dyea Canyon, was a tremendous climb up into the mountains, and many did not get past this first stage. After that, the dangers and difficulties they would have encountered were those described in *The Call of the Wild*. It was a journey that Jack London himself knew well.

Before reading

Here are some ways to help your students approach the story:

1 Give students the title of the book and show them the picture on the cover. Ask them to try and guess what kind of the story it is.

2 Give students a copy of the text on the back cover of the book, and of the story introduction on the first page. When they have read the texts, ask them a few questions about the story, or use the Before Reading Activities in the back of each Bookworm.

3 Use the pre-reading activity in this worksheet.

4 If there is a recording of this title, play the first few pages and stop at an interesting point.

The Call of the Wild

Pre-reading activity

Telling the story

Write the story of Buck the sledge dog that is told by the pictures.

Buck was a dog who lived in a big
house.

One day somebody stole him and
sold him to . . .

To the teacher

Aim: To familiarize students with the setting of the story by asking them to imagine how the story might develop
Time: 10–20 minutes
Organization: Give a copy of the worksheet to each student or group of students. Ask them to imagine the story that these pictures might illustrate. Ensure that they understand that it doesn't matter whether they tell a story that is similar to the actual story in the book or not. The interest will come from comparing their version with the story they finally read.

The Call of the Wild

While reading activity

What will happen next?

Which of these things do you think will happen in the story? Why? Why not?

	YES	NO	WHY?
1 Thornton says that Buck can pull four hundred kilos. Buck wins another 1,400 dollars.			
2 Thornton and his friends take the money and go to California.			
3 Thornton and his friends take the money and go to look for gold.			
4 Matthewson won't give the money to Thornton.			
5 Matthewson gives the money to Thornton but then steals it in the night.			
6 Thornton, Hans and Pete argue and fight about the money.			
7 Thornton sells Buck for 1,000 dollars.			
8 Buck returns to Mr Miller's house.			
9 Matthewson kills Buck.			
10 Thornton dies.			
11 Buck and Thornton leave the Yukon together.			
12 Thornton and his friends find a mountain of gold and become very rich.			

To the teacher

Where: At the end of Chapter 6
Aim: To encourage students to speculate about possible endings to the story
Time: 15–20 minutes
Organization: Give each student, or group of students, a copy of the worksheet. Ask them to decide whether these things will happen, and then write an answer to the Why? question. Correct predictions are not important, although it may be interesting for students to keep their worksheets and see whether or not they were right.

The Call of the Wild

After reading activity

Character posters

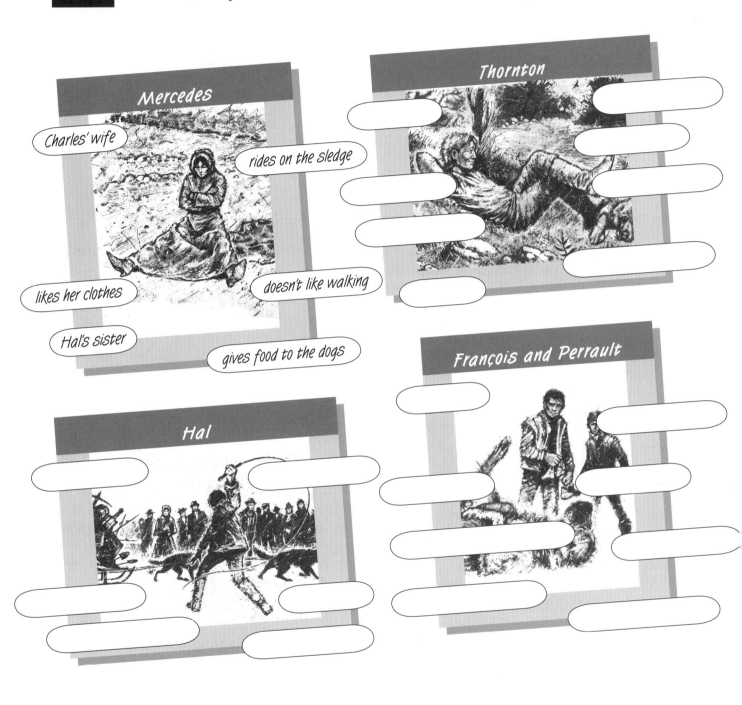

To the teacher

Aim: To focus students' attention back on the characters

Time: 20 minutes

Organization: Give each student, or group of students, a copy of the worksheet. Using the poster of Mercedes as a model, they should fill the spaces around the other pictures with appropriate words or phrases to describe the people.

The Card

Arnold Bennett

Introduction

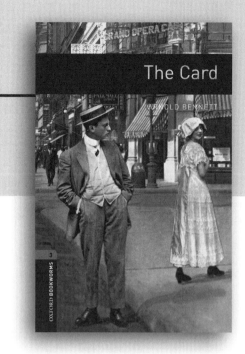

The story

The story takes place in and around Bursley, one of the Five Towns, in Staffordshire in the English Midlands. It is set at the end of the nineteenth century.

Denry (Edward Henry Machin) is the son of a poor washer-woman. By cheating in an examination at the age of twelve he gets himself into the best school in Bursley. As he grows older he is neither exactly dishonest nor is he always completely honest. But almost everything he does seems to be both successful and amusing and he gradually becomes successful, popular and rich.

His first job is working for a lawyer, Mr Duncalf. Duncalf has the job of organizing the mayor's ball, a very grand event, to which only the best people in Bursley are invited. Denry adds his own name to the list of guests, and, by giving away other free invitations, manages to get himself a new suit for the ball – and dancing lessons.

At the ball, Denry meets – and dances with – the Countess of Chell, the mayor's wife and the grandest lady in Bursley. No other man has dared to ask her to dance.

Denry has to leave Mr Duncalf's office after this, but manages to set himself up as a rent collector – a job which he manages to do very well, partly because he is prepared to lend people money – at a rate of interest – so that they can pay their rent. He starts to make a little money, and even buys a house in which an old widow lives. Then because the widow can't pay the rent, he gives her the house – a move that makes him famous and popular in the Five Towns.

One day Denry has to collect rent from Ruth, the woman who taught him to dance from the ball. She can't pay, and in the night she tries to leave the house with all her possessions. The furniture van she is using is outside the house, and it starts to roll down the hill towards the canal. Denry happens to be passing, and jumps on in an attempt to stop it. But he us unable to, and soon finds himself, still on the van, in the middle of the canal. He then discovers that Ruth is inside the van, and they are forced to spend the summer night there. The next morning they are engaged.

Ruth, her friend Nellie, and Denry go on a summer holiday to Llandudno in Wales. The holiday is very expensive, mainly because Ruth spends money like water. Ruth and Nellie return to Bursley while Denry remains in Llandudno. The engagement is over.

There has been a wreck off the coast at Llandudno, followed by a brave rescue by some lifeboatmen. Denry buys the old lifeboat and employs some of the lifeboatmen, and some of the rescued sailors, to take sightseers out into the bay to see the wreck. The enterprise is successful and Denry is soon rich.

Denry has a number of other adventures and manages to persuade the Countess to help him in another of his projects – a savings club. He also manages to persuade his mother to move from her old house to a splendid modern house outside the town.

At the end of the story, Denry is happily married to Nellie, he is going to be the next mayor of Bursley – and he is still only thirty-three years old.

Background to the story

Arnold Bennett (1867–1931) was one of the most successful British novelists of the twentieth century. He was born and brought up in Hanley, one of the Five Towns. These towns now form the city of Stoke-on-Trent and the area was, and still is, famous as a centre for the manufacture of pottery. Bennett was born into a modest family (although not as poor as Denry's) and many of his books and short stories show the life of the ordinary people of the Five Towns, from the poorest, through the middle classes, to the rich factory owners.

The Card

Pre-reading activity

Match the words with the pictures

 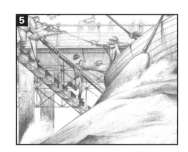 

a   The conversation was short, loud, and not very polite.

b   'Have you finished?' asked Denry.

c   Denry looked around the empty room, and then wrote a 2 in front of the 7.

d   Denry got his feet wet helping the sailors from the lifeboat onto the pier.

e   'You do pick things up easily, don't you?' said the countess.

f   Denry managed to turn the mule into Birches Street.

g   Suddenly Ruth stopped speaking, and lay back with her eyes closed.

h   Mrs Machin had never seen electric light before.

To the teacher

Aim: To familiarize students with the story and its characters

Time: 5–10 minutes

Organization: Give one copy of the worksheet to each student or each group of students (this activity can work very well in pairs). Ask the students to match each picture with the correct caption. When the students have matched the captions with the pictures you may want to ask them their ideas about what sort of person Denry is.

Key: 1c, 2e, 3a, 4g, 5d, 6f, 7h, 8b.

The Card

While reading activity

Who's going to do what?

Who is going to do which of these things in the next chapters?
Join the names to the things which happen.

1 Denry

2 Mrs Machin

3 The Countess

4 Ruth

5 Nellie

a gets a new house

b marries Ruth

c marries Nellie

d marries Denry

e becomes very rich

f loses a lot of money

g goes to live in another country

h becomes famous

i is very happy

j is very unhappy

k discovers something bad about Denry

l has an argument with Denry

m ....

n ....

To the teacher

Where: At the end of Chapter 5
Aim: To give the students the chance to predict where the story is going
Time: 10–15 minutes
Organization: Give each student, or group of students

a copy of the worksheet. Tell them that they must link the names with one or more of the sentences next to them. Any name can be joined to any sentence. The students can also write in their own ideas for sentences *m* and *n*.

The Card

After reading activity

Who, what, where and when?

Fill in the spaces.

WHO (OR WHAT)	WHERE	WHEN
Mr Duncalf	gave Denry a job	when he was sixteen.
	made a suit for Denry	
	gave Denry five pounds	
		at the ball.
Mrs Codleyn		
	gave Mrs Hullins her house	
		in the middle of a July night.
	went to Llandudno	
The *Hjalmar*		
		when Denry said 'Rothschild,' in the bookshop.
Mrs Machin	was very surprised	
	took the Countess of Chell	
	won the battle with the salt water	
Nellie		
	bought a footballer	

To the teacher

Aim: To consolidate comprehension of the story
Time: 15–20 minutes

Organization: Give each student, or group of students, a copy of the worksheet. Ask them to add as much information as possible in the blank spaces.

Chemical Secret

Tim Vicary

Introduction

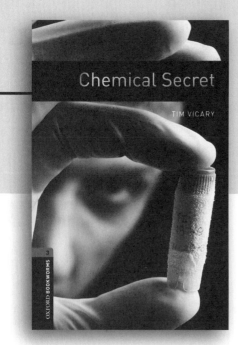

The story

John Duncan is a biologist. At the beginning of the story he gets a job with a paint company. His job is to ensure that the chemicals used in the company are safe.

John is a widower, and he lives with his two children, thirteen-year-old Andrew, and sixteen-year-old Christine. For two years he has been unemployed, and getting this job makes a big difference to both him and his children. The family move into a house by the river, near the paint factory. They can go out in their boat and look at the seals on the sandbank near the mouth of the river.

But John discovers that some of the chemicals from the factory are polluting the river. These chemicals are particularly dangerous – they can cause deformities in baby rats, and perhaps in people. He points this out to the company, but it would be very expensive to stop the pollution – too expensive. John has a choice: either he tells the newspapers about his discovery – and loses his job, or he keeps quiet, and keeps his job. He chooses to keep quiet.

But after some years the pollution does start to cause problems, and these problems are published in articles in the local newspaper, written by Simon, a journalist who is engaged to John's daughter Christine. It is not enough for John to keep quiet: now he has to start telling lies, to say that there is no pollution problem.

Christine and Simon become involved in a campaign against the factory, and one day, demonstrating from a small boat in the river, Christine, who is pregnant, falls in, and is nearly drowned. At a Public Inquiry into the pollution, John is forced to admit that there is a serious problem – and that his daughter's baby is at risk.

At the end of the story, John has lost his job – and Christine will no longer speak to him. And neither he, nor we, know whether her baby is healthy or not.

Background to the story

The story has two central themes. Firstly, it looks at the problems of pollution and of the responsibility of the businesses that cause it. Secondly, it looks at the position of an individual, where personal morality is in conflict with personal security. John has been without work for several years at the beginning of the story, and he is delighted to find a job; particularly because this now means his children can have a better life. As he starts to discover the dangers of the pollution, he is put in a terrible dilemma – and chooses to ignore the dangers in order to preserve his own, and his children's, way of life. But just keeping quiet is not enough, he is forced to start telling lies – until the day when his house of cards collapses, and he is left with nothing.

Before reading

Here are some ways to help your students approach the story:

1 Give students the title of the book and show them the picture on the cover. Ask them to try and guess what kind of the story it is.

2 Give students a copy of the text on the back cover of the book, and of the story introduction on the first page. When they have read the texts, ask them a few questions about the story, or use the Before Reading Activities in the back of each Bookworm.

3 Use the pre-reading activity in this worksheet.

4 If there is a recording of this title, play the first few pages and stop at an interesting point.

Chemical Secret

Pre-reading activity

Match the words with the pictures

a 'It's a group of seal families. The mothers come here every year to have their babies.'

b Only five metres to go now.

c 'Where do you think we can find two million pounds?'

d It was a big, comfortable house, and its gardens went down to the river.

e 'We're going to be rich . . .!'

f For two hours John had sat by the telephone, afraid to ring the hospital again.

g 'These waste products are dangerous! We've got to stop putting them in the river!'

h 'I'm eighteen! I want to get married!' said Christine.

To the teacher

Aim: To familiarize students with the story and its setting

Time: 10–15 minutes

Organization: Give one copy of the worksheet to each student or each group of students. Ask them to match the words with the appropriate picture. When the students have completed this task, check the answers with them. Then, ask them to put the pictures into the order they might appear in the story. It is not important for them to get the order correct. The important thing is to suggest an order which makes sense of the pictures. Some students may notice that one character, John, appears in most of the pictures, but gets progressively older.

Key: 1d, 2g, 3e, 4f, 5b, 6a, 7h, 8c.

Chemical Secret

While reading activity

What will happen next?

Which of these things do you think will happen in the story?

	WILL HAPPEN	MAY HAPPEN	WON'T HAPPEN	YOUR OWN COMMENTS
John will leave the paint factory.				
John will tell the newspapers about the chemicals.				
John will find a way to stop the chemicals going into the river.				
Some baby seals in the river will be born with no eyes and ears.				
The factory will close.				
The factory will spend two million pounds on machines to clean up the waste products.				
Mary will leave the factory.				
Mary will tell the newspapers about the chemicals.				
John will stay at the factory and get a lot more money.				
Mary will stay at the factory and get a lot more money.				
David Wilson will leave the factory and Mary will get his job.				
David Wilson will leave the factory and John will get his job.				
The factory will get bigger, and more waste products will go into the river.				
John will marry Mary.				
(Your suggestion)				

To the teacher

Where: At the end of Chapter 6
Aim: To encourage students to predict the development of the story
Time: 10–15 minutes
Organization: Give each student, or group of students, a copy of the worksheet. Ask them to

discuss in groups and decide, without looking beyond the end of Chapter 6, what will happen as the story unfolds. It is not important whether their predictions are correct, although it may be interesting for students to keep their worksheets and see whether or not they were right.

Chemical Secret
After reading activity

Character crosswords

Look at the character crossword for John.

```
NEEDS A (J)OB
    A BI|O|LOGIST
        |H|URTS HIS LEG
NEEDS MO(N)EY
```

Make similar 'crosswords' for some of the other characters.

```
.....................M.....................
.....................A.....................              .....................W.....................
.....................R.....................              .....................I.....................
.....................Y.....................              .....................L.....................
                                                         .....................S.....................
.....................C.....................              .....................O.....................
.....................H.....................              .....................N.....................
.....................R.....................
.....................I.....................              .....................S.....................
.....................S.....................              .....................I.....................
.....................T.....................              .....................M.....................
.....................I.....................              .....................O.....................
.....................A.....................              .....................N.....................
.....................N.....................
```

To the teacher

Aim: To revise characters
Time: 20–30 minutes

Organization: Give each student, or group of students, a copy of the worksheet and ask them to make character crosswords as in the example.

© OXFORD UNIVERSITY PRESS **PHOTOCOPIABLE**

A Christmas Carol

Charles Dickens

Introduction

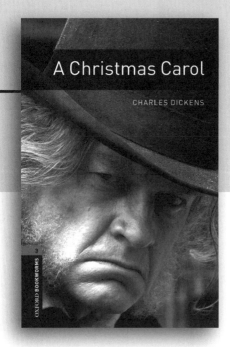

The story

Scrooge is a mean old man who lives a secretive and lonely life. The only thing that matters to him is making money and he takes no interest at all in other people. For the last seven years Scrooge has run his business alone since the death of his partner Jacob Marley. Scrooge works in a dark, cold office with his clerk, Bob Cratchit, who is treated badly and paid very little.

One cold foggy Christmas Eve, Scrooge has several visitors at his office. His nephew comes to wish him 'Merry Christmas' and invite him to dinner. Scrooge angrily rejects the invitation and says that Christmas is 'humbug' - a complete nonsense. Two gentlemen then arrive collecting money for the poor. Scrooge refuses to give money, sends the visitors away and shuts the office. On arriving home Scrooge is visited by the ghost of Jacob Marley. Jacob explains that because he did not help others in life he has to travel endlessly through the world without peace or rest. The same will happen to Scrooge if he does not change. Jacob says that three spirits will visit Scrooge over the following days.

The first spirit is the ghost of Christmas Past. The ghost is half child, half man, with long white hair and a light that shines from the top of his head. Scrooge travels with the ghost back into his past. At first he sees himself as a lonely schoolboy with a cruel father, then there is his loving sister who dies, leaving behind his nephew. Next there is a lively Christmas party given by Scrooge's former boss, the kind Mr Fezziwig. Finally, Scrooge sees his former fiancee, Belle, who left him because he was only interested in money. These scenes make him cry. He cannot bear more of these memories and suddenly finds himself back in bed again.

The second visitor is the ghost of Christmas Present. This friendly spirit takes Scrooge to see Christmas dinner at Bob Cratchit's house. Although the Cratchit family are poor, they are grateful and loving. The spirit tells Scrooge that Tiny Tim, Bob's disabled son, will soon die if his life does not change. Scrooge is horrified. Scrooge then visits the house of his nephew, Fred, where everybody is playing games and laughing cheerfully about Uncle Scrooge.

Finally, Scrooge meets the spirit of Christmas Yet to Come. This ghost is tall and silent with a long black robe which hides its head and body. Scrooge is most afraid of this spirit but he is keen to learn how to change his life. They travel to the future and see people talking about a mean old man who has died alone. Scrooge discovers that this sad, lonely, old man is himself and that Tiny Tim is dead. Scrooge promises to change and to keep Christmas forever in his heart.

The next day Scrooge jumps out of bed a changed man. It is still Christmas day. He is so excited at the thought of changing his future that he rushes around wishing people 'Merry Christmas'. He sends a large turkey to Bob Cratchit's house, gives money to the poor and spends all afternoon with his nephew playing party games. After Christmas Scrooge pays Bob twice as much and he becomes a second father to Tiny Tim, who doesn't die. Scrooge lives a happy, generous life and the spirits never visit him again.

Background to the story

Charles Dickens (1812–70) was a major English writer of novels, many of which are set against the harsh conditions of Victorian England. His other novels in the Oxford Bookworms Series include: *A Tale of Two Cities, David Copperfield, Great Expectations* and *Oliver Twist.*

A Christmas Carol

Pre-reading activity

Match the words with the pictures

a The knocker had become the face of Jacob Marley!

b 'Do you, Ebeneezer Scrooge, recognize my chain?'

c 'He hasn't left his money to me,' said the fat man.

d 'A merry Christmas, Bob!' said Scrooge.'

e Scrooge kept his door open to check that Bob Cratchit was working.

f Scrooge stared at his ghostly visitor.

g Both names still stood above the office door.

h The spirit pointed down at one of the graves.

To the teacher

Aim: To introduce students to the story and its principal characters

Time: 25 minutes

Organization: Give one copy of the worksheet to each student, or to each group of students. Ask the students to match the picture with the correct caption.

Key: 1b, 2e, 3h, 4d, 5a, 6g, 7f, 8c. When they have done this ask them the following questions:

1 Which character in the pictures is Scrooge? What adjectives could they use to describe him? (old, ugly ...) Which character is Bob Cratchit? What is his relationship with Scrooge?

2 What is the date of this story? What type of story is it?

3 What do the ghosts say to Scrooge?

4 Which illustration comes at the end of the book? Why?

It is not important for students to get the right answers to these questions.

A Christmas Carol

While reading activity

Word grid

Find the answers to the clues below and fill in the word grid. When you have finished you will find the name of a person, which runs through the middle of all the words. The first has been done for you.

1 'If I hear another sound from *you*,' said Scrooge, 'you'll lose your _____!'

2 The ghost wears this around its middle.

3 Scrooge sees the face of a ghost on this thing.

4 Scrooge has white _____ on his head, his eyebrows and his chin.

5 The small office where Bob Cratchit works.

6 Scrooge's favourite expression.

7 Bob Cratchit wears this to keep himself warm.

8 Every tile on the _____ has a picture of a ghost's face.

9 Bob Cratchit's job.

10 Scrooge isn't generous but very _____.

11 Scrooge doesn't _____ Bob very much.

		1 J	O	B

Where: At the end of Chapter 1

Aim: To help revise vocabulary and key events

Time: 20 minutes

Organization: Give each student, or pair of students a copy of the grid and look at the first example together as a class. Ask the students to read the clues and find the other missing words. When they have done all the questions they will find the name of a person (Jacob Marley) which runs through the words. When everyone has finished, go through the answers as a class.

Key: 1 job, 2 chain, 3 knocker, 4 frost, 5 cupboard, 6 humbug, 7 scarf, 8 fireplace, 9 clerk, 10 mean, 11 pay.

A Christmas Carol

After reading activity

Complete the grid

NAME	DESCRIPTION	SAYS	TAKES SCROOGE TO
Jacob Marley's Ghost			
The Ghost of Christmas Past			
The Ghost of Christmas Present			
The Ghost of Christmas Future			

Description

1 A tall, silent figure with a long black robe which hides its head and body.
2 A friendly, smiling spirit with long brown hair and a torch in its hand.
3 A ghost with death-cold eyes and a long chain with money-boxes around its middle.
4 A figure which is half child, half man with long white hair, soft skin and a bright light shining from the top of its head.

Says

5 'In the future I see an empty chair by the fire, with a crutch beside it.
If these shadows do not change, the child will die.'
6 'No peace, no rest for me in death, because I was never kind or good in life.'
7 'Not everyone has left the school ... There is one lonely child there still ...'
8 Nothing.

Takes Scrooge to

9 A shop which sells old furniture and clothes.
10 Mr Fezziwig's Christmas party.
11 A lively Christmas party at his nephew's house.
12 His own grave.
13 The town where he was born.
14 A lighthouse.

To the teacher

Aim: To focus students' attention back on the different ghosts
Time: 30 minutes
Organization: As a class, ask students how many ghosts there were in the story and how much they can remember about each one. Then give each student, or group of students a copy of the chart. Ask them to identify which answers at the bottom go with which ghost or spirit. Go through the answers as a class.
Key: Jacob Marley's ghost: 3, 6. The ghost of Christmas Past: 4, 7, 10, 13. The ghost of Christmas Present: 2, 5, 11, 14. The ghost of Christmas Future: 1, 8, 9, 12.
Then ask the students the following questions:

1 How does Scrooge's attitude change as he meets each of the ghosts? Why? Possible answer: At first he has a very negative attitude towards the ghosts but then he realises he can learn how to change his life from them.
2 Which ghost is he most afraid of? Why? Possible answer: The ghost of Christmas Future. Because he is afraid of what the future might hold for him.

The Crown of Violet

Geoffrey Trease

Introduction

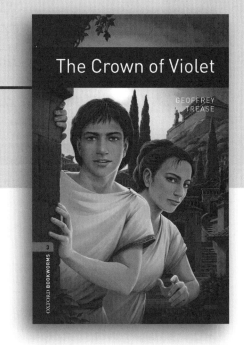

The Crown of Violet

GEOFFREY TREASE

OXFORD BOOKWORMS

The story

The story is set in the Greek city-state of Athens in the fifth century BC. Athens is famous for its Theatre Festival and the hill of the Acropolis – the city's crown of violet stone. Although there is a system of democracy, girls and women have to stay at home, and can't talk to men or discuss politics.

A boy called Alexis wakes up excitedly on the morning of the Theatre Festival which he attends with his family. There, he pokes fun at Hippias, an unpleasant man, and makes an enemy.

After the festival Alexis and his friend Lucian meet Corinna, a girl who plays the flute. She shows them her secret cave. Alexis immediately likes Corinna but Lucian looks down on her; she isn't a real Athenian and lives alone in an inn with her mother who cooks. Although born in Athens, Corinna was brought up in Athens.

One night when Alexis and Lucian ride in a relay torch race on horseback, Alexis sees Hippias talking to a mysterious gentleman with deep eyes and a long nose. They are obviously planning something. During the race Alexis nearly drops the torch and consequently falls out with Lucian who is also jealous of Corinna.

The following day Alexis meets Corinna at the house of Cephalus, the sculptor. Alexis sees a sculpture of the mysterious man with deep eyes – it is Magnes who has been exiled for planning a revolution. He is a danger to democracy in Athens and will be killed if found in the city. Alexis tells Lucian, who informs his uncle on the City Council. The Council don't believe Magnes is in Athens and say that everything is under control. Alexis begins to question the ideas of adults and starts to listen to the wise but controversial Socrates, which angers his father. Alexis and Corinna continue their friendship but meet secretly because she is a girl.

Alexis writes a comedy called *The Gadfly* which puts the ideas of Socrates in a positive light. Because Alexis is young he asks his great Uncle Paintbrush to enter the play for the Theatre Festival and to their surprise it is accepted. Alexis and Paintbrush go to see the minister for plays who understands that it is really Alexis who has written it. The cost of the play will be met by a rich man called Conon. Conon and his wife once had a child the same age as Alexis.

Alexis and Corinna find a secret message at the cave and guess that the final plans for a revolution will be made at a party at Hippias' house. Corrina's mother, Gorgo, is cooking for the party and Corinna goes along as a flute player. She learns that Hippias and Magnes are planning to strike at the time of the Festival.

Alexis follows Hippias to the secret cave on the night before the festival where he learns that the revolution will take place the following evening. Alexis is caught and tied up but is rescued by Lucian and Corinna.

On the day of the Theatre Festival Alexis tells an Athenian general about the revolution. Alexis puts a secret warning into his play which means that all the enemies of Athens stand up and walk out, only to be caught by Athenian soldiers.

The Gadfly wins first prize and everybody realises that Alexis really wrote it. Through watching the play Alexis' father also learns to respect the ideas of Socrates. Finally, it turns out that Corinna is the daughter of Conan and a real Athenian after all.

Background to the story

Geoffrey Trease (1909–1998) was an English writer of plays, short stories, translations, poems and biographies but his best-known books are his many historical adventure stories for young people.

STAGE 3

The Crown of Violet
Pre-reading activity

Match the words with the pictures

a   Corinna jumped wildly into the-tree.
b   'This is my seat,' the young man-said. 'You'll have to move.'
c   'Don't try to escape,' Magnes said.
d   'Someone's been here. There are-footprints in the snow.'
e   'Yes, my boy, that's one of my best statues.'
f   Glaucus stepped forward and began his speech.
g   'She looks just like you, when you-were younger.'
h   Alexis saw the face of the stranger.

The Crown of Violet
While reading activity

What will happen next?

Which of these things do you think will happen in the story?

	WILL HAPPEN	MAY HAPPEN	WON'T HAPPEN	YOUR OWN COMMENTS
The play will be accepted for the Theatre Festival.				
The play will be rejected from the Theatre Festival because they find out that a boy wrote it.				
Alexis will argue with his father about Socrates and go to live in the secret cave.				
Alexis will tell his family all about Magncs and Hippias.				
Corinna and Alexis will find a secret message with information about the plans of Hippias and Magnes.				
Corinna will play the flute at the house of Hippias and find out about his plans.				
Gorgo will try to stop Hippias and his friends by poisoning them with food at the party.				
Magnes will catch Alexis at the secret cave and tie him up.				
Corinna will find out who her real father is.				
Hippias will kill Corinna and Alexis because they know too much.				
With the help of powerful friends, Magnes will take control of Athens.				
(Your suggestion)				
(Your suggestion)				

To the teacher

Where: At the end of chapter 4
Aim: To encourage students to predict the development of the story
Time: 15 minutes
Organization: Give each student, or group of students, a copy of the worksheet. Ask them to discuss in groups and decide, without looking beyond the end of Chapter 4, what will happen as the story unfolds. It is not important whether their predictions are correct, although it may be interesting for students to keep their worksheets and see whether or not they were right.

The Crown of Violet

After reading activity

Character matching

Magnes

Uncle Paintbrush

Hippias

Alexis

Lucian

Corinna

Alexis

3

1 Is a vase painter.
2 Has two hundred long knives.
3 Writes *The Gadfly*.
4 Has deep eyes and a long nose.
5 Doesn't like Corinna.
6 Lived in Sicily.
7 Admires Socrates.
8 Is a kind, gentle man.
9 Doesn't like foreigners.
10 Has a party.

11 Wants to learn the flute.
12 Is a friend of the Spartans.
13 Has an uncle on the City Council.
14 Wants to learn to read and write.
15 Is old and forgetful.
16 Thinks democracy is a stupid idea.
17 Likes Corinna.
18 Has a mother who is a cook.

19 Pretends to write *The Gadfly*.
20 Is a gentleman dressed as a working man.
21 Wants to do sport all the time.
22 Has long hair, gold rings and high boots.
23 Decides not to kill Alexis.
24 Lives in an inn.

To the teacher

Aim: To revise descriptions of characters
Time: 20 minutes
Organization: Give the worksheets to pairs or groups of students. Ask them to match the names of characters to the pictures and then match the descriptions with the characters.

Key: a: Alexis 3, 7, 11, 17; b: Corinna 6, 14, 18, 24; c: Lucian 5, 9, 13, 21; d: Hippias 2, 10, 16, 22; e: Uncle Paintbrush 1, 8, 15, 19; f: Magnes 4, 12, 20, 23.

Dancing with Strangers: Stories from Africa

Retold by Clare West

Introduction

The stories

Ekaterina is the story of a plane ride. Neil Gordon is travelling back to his home in Johannesburg and a beautiful young girl joins the plane in Athens. She can't speak English, but they manage to communicate and Neil discovers that she has been married by proxy to a Greek man living in Johannesburg. He is suspicious of the photo of the husband, which shows him standing in front of a brand new car which is years out of date. When the plane lands in Johannesburg, the husband is indeed a much older man, and Neil gives Ekaterina his business card, hoping that she will contact him if she wants to escape from the marriage. But when the story ends, he is still waiting to hear from her.

Breaking Loose is set in Tanzania and tells the story of the friendship between Yasmin, a university student from an Indian family, and Daniel, a professor from another African country. They are attracted to each other, but there is a gulf between them, because of their different cultures. Yasmin stops meeting Daniel because of her mother's opposition, but she has been challenged by his views and she learns more about her Indian background. After her father's death, Yasmin is ready to resume her friendship with Daniel in spite of her mother.

Remember Atita describes Atita's search for her old school friends. Atita is an orphan and she left Gulu after the death of her grandfather to go and live with relatives. Gulu suffered greatly during the civil war, and the surrounding villages are still threatened by the rebels. Atita spends her days searching for her friends, and sleeps on a veranda at night with village children hiding from the rebels. Okema, who has lost all his brothers and sisters to the rebels, is her particular friend. Eventually, Atita finds one of her old friends, Laker, in the hospital. Laker does not remember her, and so Atita visits day after day, trying to restore her memory. Eventually, Laker tells her about the fate of their friend Oyella, who was captured and shot by the rebels. At last, Laker remembers Atita, and smiles.

A Gathering of Bald Men is an amusing story set in Johannesburg. It tells the story of Caleb, who is married to Nothando and the father of two daughters. Caleb is in debt and is unhappy in his job, but it is the discovery that he is starting to go bald which leads him to think of suicide. He goes to drink in a bar and becomes even more morose. Ranger (a con man, pretending to be blind) befriends him, and eventually drives him recklessly through the town and crashes into a wall. Nothando, Caleb's wife, is relieved to find that Caleb has been only slightly injured in the crash. Caleb is inspired to set up his own company, dealing with the problems of baldness, and Ranger joins him in this venture. The story ends two years later, with Caleb now a successful businessman.

Dancing with Strangers: Stories from Africa

Pre-reading activity

Picture match

Match the pictures with the words and the story titles

Words ☐ Title ☐   Words ☐ Title ☐   Words ☐ Title ☐   Words ☐ Title ☐

Words ☐ Title ☐   Words ☐ Title ☐   Words ☐ Title ☐   Words ☐ Title ☐

Words

a The streets were crowded. Caleb looked at everything and tried to remember it for ever.

b We sit on the veranda because it's safer to spend the night in the town.

c A bewildered little group of men and women came into the airport building.

d The Matumbi was a tea shop under a tree.

e It was a dance that did not need any closeness or touching.

f I avoided her eyes, pouring more wine into our glasses.

g I watch her face and wait, hoping for a smile which will tell me that she knows me.

h He had discovered a bald patch and he was very miserable about it.

Story Titles (use each title twice)

i Ekaterina

j Breaking Loose

k Remember Atita

l A Gathering of Bald Men

To the teacher

Aim: To encourage students to predict the setting and themes of the four stories

Time: 30 minutes

Organization: Put the students into pairs after they have read the cover and the introduction. Give one copy of the worksheet to each pair. Ask them to discuss and predict which story belongs to which picture, and then add the words to the pictures. They may need to use a dictionary to check some of the more unusual words. Check the answers with the whole class. The important thing is to begin thinking about the stories, not the accuracy of the answers.

Key: 1ej, 2fi, 3al, 4bk, 5ci, 6hl, 7gk, 8dj

Dancing with Strangers: Stories from Africa

While reading activity

Getting it right

Correct as many mistakes as possible.

Yesterday I went to The Matumbi with ~~my father~~ *Daniel*. I had my first sikisti. It's a cold egg sandwich. It's called sikisti because it costs twenty cents. I talked to Daniel about my family. I talked about my father's pawnshop, and his shop which makes women's clothes. Today Daniel came to the shop. He wanted to look at the new gramophones. He went into the house and met my father. I went inside the house and talked to my mother. She was very angry because Daniel is not African. 'He's a salesman!' I said. But father never stops warning me, and punishing me, and expecting the worst just because I'm a girl! My sisters never have this problem! She went on shouting and screaming for hours. By the end of the day I felt half dead with tiredness. I am not going to the end-of-year university because of her!

To the teacher

Where: At the end of Breaking Loose
Aim: To help with summarizing and revision of Breaking Loose
Time: 30 minutes
Organization: Give out the extract from Yasmin's diary, written after Daniel visits her father's shop. There are eleven factual mistakes in it and the first one has been corrected as an example. Ask the students, or pairs of students, to change the mistakes. When everybody has finished, go through the answers as a class and then ask the students to write a diary extract from the point of view of either Daniel or Yasmin's mother.

Key: cold: *hot*; twenty: *sixty*; women's: *men's*; new: *old*; house: *shop*; African: *Asian*; salesman: *professor*; father: *mother*; sisters: *brothers*; university: *dance*

Dancing with Strangers: Stories from Africa

After reading activity

Match the words and phrases with each of the three characters

Put these words or phrases next to the most appropriate person.

pink Renault	a beauty that was centuries old	hangman	bus company	
scar under chin	Gulu hospital	Marcia	Gordon	Won Okech
professor of sociology	trainers	laughing wildly, crazily	reads about India	
new wedding ring	president	PHEW	my business card	
unfashionable old things	afraid of thunder	torn blue blanket		

	WORDS/PHRASES	WHAT ABOUT
Ekaterina		
Neil		
Yasmin		
Daniel		
Atita		
Laker		
Okema		
Caleb		
Nothando		
Ranger		

To the teacher

Aim: To focus students' attention on the characters of the four stories

Time: 30 minutes

Organization: Give each student, or pair of students, a copy of the chart and ask them to identify which word or phrase goes with each character. Go through the answers as a class and then ask students to talk more about the characters.

Key: Ekaterina: a beauty that was centuries old (her appearance), new wedding ring (she is wearing this); Neil: Gordon (surname), business card (gives this to Ekaterina); Yasmin: literature (she is studying this at university), reads about India (she does this during the holidays); Daniel: professor of sociology (his job), unfashionable old things (he likes these); Atita: scar under chin (where she fell off seesaw), Won Okech (her grandfather); Laker: laughing wildly, crazily (after she has told Atita about Oyella), torn blue blanket (covers her in Gulu hospital); Okema: afraid of thunder (because there was thunder when the rebels came), president (wants to be President and end the war); Caleb: pink Renault (his car), PHEW (name of new company); Nothando: bus company (place where she works), Marcia (her friend); Ranger: trainers (his shoes); hangman (his father was one)

STAGE 3

Ethan Frome

Edith Wharton

Introduction

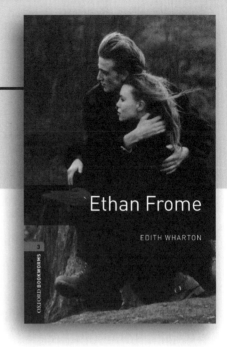

This ungraded summary is for the teacher's use only and should not be given to students.

The story

The narrator of the story goes to live for a time in the isolated town of Starkfield, Massachusetts. While he is there, he meets Ethan Frome, a poor farmer of fifty-two with a twisted body. He learns the sad story of Ethan's life.

As a young man, more than twenty years earlier, Ethan lived with his wife, Zeena, and her cousin, Mattie Silver. Zeena was a cold woman, who was interested only in her own ill-health, and not Ethan, who fell in love with her warm and vivacious cousin – and she with him. Mattie was a poor orphan, with nowhere to live, and she had come to stay with the Fromes and to look after the house because Zeena was unwell.

Zeena, however, became aware of the growing love between her husband and her cousin, and decided that Mattie would have to leave – the Fromes had very little money, and she pointed out that they couldn't afford to keep her. For a while, Ethan wondered whether he should take Mattie and run off with her to the West. But he didn't have enough money for the train fare. He could get the money by borrowing from his friends – but did not want to take advantage of them – there would be no escape for Ethan.

On the day of Mattie's departure Ethan took her to the station by sleigh. At the top of a hill, they found a sled which somebody had forgotten, and Ethan suggested they have one last ride. His intention was to steer the sled into a tree and kill them both, but he failed. Both he and Mattie were very badly injured.

One night, in a snowstorm, the narrator finds himself at the Fromes' farm. Ethan is living there in poverty, with two sick, complaining women – Mattie and Zeena.

Background to the story

Ethan Frome, first published in 1911, is set in the cold and forbidding environment of New England at the turn of the twentieth century. It was a surprising subject for Edith Wharton to choose for what is probably her greatest tragic novel. Most of her novels and short stories show the rich and aristocratic of Europe and North America – a society which she knew well, both from her youth in New York, and from her life in France, where she lived from 1907. But, in fact, in a very different environment, it looks at something which Wharton was particularly interested in – the way in which the conventions of the community can hold an individual, and stop them achieving their happiness.

Wharton wrote a large number of short stories, as well as novels and poetry, and, finding herself in France during the First World War, was also drawn into war work which reflected itself in some of her later writing.

Before reading

Here are some ways to help your students approach the story:

1   Give students the title of the book and show them the picture on the cover. Ask them to try and guess what kind of the story it is.

2   Give students a copy of the text on the back cover of the book, and of the story introduction on the first page. When they have read the texts, ask them a few questions about the story, or use the Before Reading Activities in the back of each Bookworm.

3   Use the pre-reading activity in this worksheet.

4   If there is a recording of this title, play the first few pages and stop at an interesting point.

Ethan Frome
Pre-reading activity

Match the words with the pictures

a The kitchen was warm and welcoming.
b It was where they had sat once last August . . .
c Ethan looked at his wife with eyes full of hate.
d Zeena was eating well, and seemed very lively and busy.
e There were two women sitting there.
f 'I've been in a dream,' thought Ethan.
g 'I thought you weren't coming back!' Mattie cried.
h 'Oh, Ethan, what will Zeena say? It was her very best dish!'

To the teacher

Aim: To familiarize students with the story and its setting
Time: 5–10 minutes
Organization: Give one copy of the worksheet to each student or each group of students. Ask the students to match the words with the appropriate picture. When the students have completed this task, check the answers with them. Then, ask them to identify the three characters, Ethan, Mattie and Zeena and the nature of the relationship between the three of them.
Key: 1c, 2g, 3a, 4f, 5b, 6e, 7h, 8d.

Ethan Frome

While reading activity

What will happen next?

Which of these things do you think will happen in the story?

ETHAN	YES/NO
will ask Mattie to leave Starkfield.	
will ask Mattie to run away with him.	
will ask Zeena for a divorce.	
will try to kill Zeena.	
will leave Starkfield alone.	
will go and live in Florida.	
will try to kill himself and Mattie.	
(none of these)	

ZEENA	YES/NO
will stay in Bettsbridge with her aunt.	
will die.	
will discover Ethan and Mattie kissing.	
will make Mattie leave the house.	
will ask Ethan for a divorce.	
will get better.	
(none of these)	

MATTIE	YES/NO
will ask Ethan to run away with her.	
will try and kill herself.	
will leave Starkfield.	
will try and kill Zeena.	
will marry Denis Eady.	
(none of these)	

To the teacher

Where: At the end of Chapter 4

Aim: To encourage students to predict the development of the story

Time: 10–15 minutes

Organization: Give each student, or group of students, a copy of the worksheet. Ask them to decide, without looking beyond the end of Chapter 4, what will happen to each of the three main characters. Correct predictions are not important, although it may be interesting for students to keep their worksheets and see whether or not they were right.

 © OXFORD UNIVERSITY PRESS

Ethan Frome
After reading activity

Character posters

♠♥♦♣ MATTIE ♠♥♦♣

dark-haired

warm and smiling

no friends or money

loves beauty

white skin and dark eyes

had a rich father

never studied or learnt a job

not strong

♠♥♦♣ ETHAN ♠♥♦♣

♠♥♦♣ ZEENA ♠♥♦♣

To the teacher

Aim: To focus students' attention back on the characters
Time: 20 minutes

Organization: Give each student, or group of students, a copy of the worksheet. Let them look at the example of the poster of Mattie. They should then finish the posters of Zeena and Ethan.

Frankenstein

Mary Shelley

Introduction

The story

The novel begins with Swiss scientist, Victor Frankenstein, being rescued by a ship at the North Pole. He tells the story of how he tried to create life to help people, and the terrible consequences of his experiments . . .

Victor went to university where he studied electricity and succeeded in putting life into a human form, made of dead body parts. This ugly new creature saw Victor as his master, but the scientist was horrified and abandoned him. The poor monster wanted to be loved but he soon learned that people were afraid of his size and appearance.

From watching a family, he learned to speak and read. He was secretly kind to the family and felt he could trust them. One day, he revealed himself but they were afraid and attacked him. He understood that his life would always be unhappy and he felt full of hate for Victor, his creator.

The monster decided to find Victor and, by chance, he met Victor's little brother, William. Wanting to hurt Victor, he killed William and implicated the family's nanny, Justine, by placing a gold chain on her. Justine was arrested and killed.

Victor went to the mountains to recover. The monster found him and said how unhappy and lonely he felt. Victor listened and agreed to make the monster a female companion. However, later he realized that this was a mistake and destroyed the creature. The monster was very angry and promised to ruin Victor's life. He then killed Victor's best friend and his bride, Elizabeth. Victor's father died as a result.

Victor wanted to kill the monster and followed him to the North Pole where he dies from the cold just after telling his story to the ship's captain. The monster finds Victor's body and is very sad at the death of his creator. He promises to kill himself, saying that he only wanted love and friendship.

Background to the story

Frankenstein was written while Mary Shelley (1797–1851) was travelling through Europe with her husband, Percy Bysshe Shelley, the Romantic poet. The descriptions of towns and countryside in the novel come from this trip.

One stormy night when they were staying with Lord Byron at his villa near Geneva, it was suggested that they individually write a ghost story. At first Mary could not think of a story but later she had a powerful vision of a monster and so *Frankenstein* was born. She was only 19 years old.

The novel is in the Gothic literary tradition – a tale of supernatural events set in a wild landscape. The full title, *Frankenstein: or, the Modern Prometheus*, refers to the mythological figure who stole fire from the gods to create man and animals.

Mary Shelley was pregnant when writing the novel. Two of her children had already died young. The novel can also be seen as an examination of fears and thoughts about pregnancy, childbirth and child development.

There have been more films made of the novel than any other book. The majority have a stereotyped 'evil' monster and a 'mad' scientist. Clearly, this is a highly limited view which fails to understand Victor, the monster and their tragic relationship.

Frankenstein
Pre-reading activity

True or False?

For each of the sentences about Frankenstein, mark one of the columns.

		TRUE	FALSE	DON'T KNOW
1	Frankenstein is the name of the monster.			
2	The monster is very large.			
3	The monster learns about the Greeks and Romans.			
4	The monster has a wife.			
5	The monster can speak English.			
6	The scientist loves the creature he creates.			
7	The monster is evil from the beginning.			
8	The monster needs blood to live.			

To the teacher

Aim: To raise interest in the story
Time: 10 minutes
Organization: Write the word Frankenstein on the board or show the front cover of the book to the class. Ask the students what they know about the story. Then divide the class into pairs and give one worksheet between each pair. Ask each pair to discuss the statements and to tick whether each statement is true, false, or not known. Go through the students' ideas as a class and encourage students to say why they have chosen a certain answer. Do not focus on whether the answers are correct or not as students will find out when they read the book. Generate as much discussion as possible and encourage students to share their ideas.

Frankenstein

While reading activity 1

Hidden word

Read the clues and find the different words that come from Frankenstein. *When you have done this, find the name of a person that runs down through the middle of all of the other words.*

Clues

1 The living thing that Frankenstein makes.
2 The power that Frankenstein uses to make the monster come to life.
3 The woman who goes to prison for murder.
4 The country where Frankenstein was born.
5 The person who is strangled by the monster.

6 The place where Frankenstein makes the monster.
7 Frankenstein's best friend who comes to visit him.
8 Frankenstein sees a tree destroyed by this.
9 The police find this in a coat pocket.

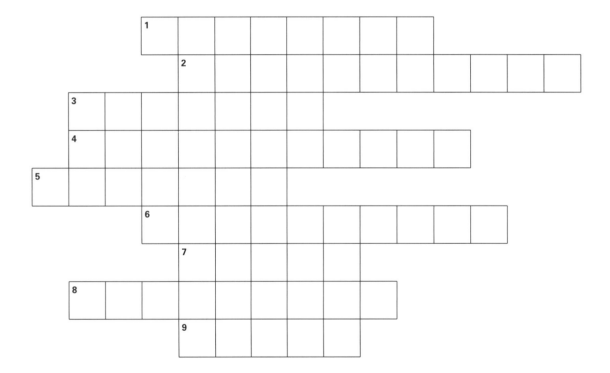

Where: At the end of Chapter 6
Aim: To revise some of the main characters and events
Time: 30 minutes
Organization: Give each student, or pair of students a copy of the word quiz. They need to read the clues and find the nine words. By doing this, they will find the missing word that runs through all of the other words. Go through the answers as a class and see

how much the students can remember about the characters whose names are in the quiz.

When this is finished ask the students to write a dialogue in which Frankenstein tells Elizabeth what he has done. Write the first few lines of the dialogue as a class. The activity should help students to focus on events so far in the book and the reasons why Frankenstein created a monster.

STAGE 3

Frankenstein
While reading activity 2

Matching quotations to the speaker

Who says the following things in Frankenstein?

QUOTATION	VICTOR	MONSTER	WHAT IS HAPPENING?
1 'I learnt to love and to be patient were the most important things in the world.'	✓		*Victor is talking about his happy childhood.*
2 'I am the unhappiest creature in the world but I shall fight for my life.'			
3 'Day after day, month after month I followed death.'			
4 'You are a murderer. How can I be kind to you?'			
5 'I learnt that people think it is very important to have money and to come from a good family.'			
6 'I did not know then that my work would destroy me and the people that I loved.'			
7 'Now is the time! Save me and help me!'			
8 'At first my eyes and ears did not work very well, but after a while I began to see and hear clearly.'			
9 'I was filled with fear at what I had done.'			
10 'Come with me to a warmer place, and listen to my story. Then you can decide.'			

To the teacher

Where: At the end of Chapter 8
Aim: To recap key events and emotions in the story
Time: 15 minutes
Organization: Divide the class into groups and give one worksheet between each group. Ask the students to decide whether the statements below were made by Victor Frankenstein or the monster. Encourage them also to discuss how these statements fit into the story. When the students have finished, go through the answers as a class and generate discussion about how the statements fit into the story.

Key: 1 Victor, 2 Monster, 3 Victor, 4 Victor, 5 Monster, 6 Victor, 7 Monster, 8 Monster, 9 Victor, 10 Monster.

Frankenstein

After reading activity

Victor Frankenstein: Hero or Villain?

· ·

Opinion A

· ·

I think Victor Frankenstein was a good man who should have
our sympathy. He tried to create life because he wanted to
help people. He was a brilliant scientist and, with hard work,
he was successful in creating life. To make a better world
scientists must experiment. Sadly, for Victor, his creation was
an evil monster. We should feel sorry for Victor because the
monster destroyed everything he loved. Victor tried to kill the
monster to protect other people and he died in the process. We
should be pleased that Victor was not a bad man who used the
monster to hurt others.

· ·

Opinion B

· ·

I cannot agree that Victor Frankenstein was a good man. He
was a bad scientist because he created life without thinking of
what would happen. Then, he ran away from his creation and
left it alone in a world where people were frightened of it. The
monster was not born bad and dangerous but he became evil
because of Victor's actions. Victor did not love his creation and
he never realized that this was his biggest mistake. Because the
monster didn't have a father, he didn't know how to behave. In
short, I believe that Victor was responsible for the death and
destruction of his own family.

To the teacher

Aim: To discuss key themes in the story
Time: 30 minutes
Organization: Divide the class into two. Ask half the
class to read Opinion A and the other half to read

Opinion B. Ask the students to underline the different
points in the argument. Then put one student who has
read Opinion A with another who has read Opinion B
and ask them to argue their case.

STAGE 3

Goldfish

Raymond Chandler

Introduction

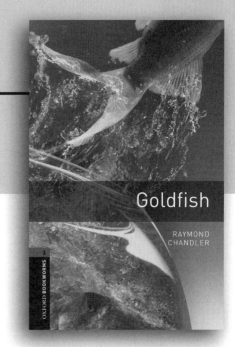

Goldfish

RAYMOND
CHANDLER

OXFORD BOOKWORMS

The story

Carmady is a private detective in Los Angeles. A friend, Kathy Horne, tells him that her lodger knows something about the Leander pearls. These were stolen 19 years ago, Kathy explains, and never recovered. The suspect, Wally Sype, was imprisoned, and then released a few years ago. Kathy's lodger, Peeler Mardo, has learnt that Sype still has the pearls and has hidden them.

Carmady visits Mardo to get more information, only to find that he has just died, apparently while being tortured. Carmady decides to look for the pearls and share with Kathy the $25,000 reward money offered by the insurance company.

Carmady isn't the only one interested in the pearls. Mardo, while drunk, had talked about them to Carol Donovan. She knows that Carmady is interested and, along with her crooked lawyer friend, Rush Madder, manages to delay Carmady and get a head start.

Carmady knows only two things about Sype: that he lives somewhere near Olympia, in northwestern America, and that he keeps goldfish.

Carmady finds Sunset, a friend of Mardo's who knows something about the pearls. He tells Carmady that Sype is living in the nearby town of Westport. The two men agree to work together, and are about to set out when Madder and Donovan find them. During an argument, Madder collapses unconscious, and Donovan shoots Sunset. Carmady manages to lock her in a bathroom, and he sets off for Westport in Sunset's car.

Carmady tracks down Sype. He denies knowing anything about the pearls and eventually pulls out a gun. Just then Donovan and Madder arrive; they have Sype's wife at gunpoint. Sype drops his gun. In the fighting that follows, Donovan tries to kill Carmady but is shot by Mrs Sype; Madder shoots Sype; and Carmady wounds Madder in the knee. Overhearing Sype's dying words to his wife, Carmady examines a pair of goldfish and discovers the pearls sewn under their skin.

While they wait for the police and doctor to arrive, Mrs Sype explains to Carmady that the pearls were fakes and asks him casually if she can have them back. Carmady almost believes her, but eventually realizes she is lying. He keeps the pearls. Half the reward money will go to him, and half to Kathy.

Background to the story

This is one of Raymond Chandler's earlier short stories, written in the 1930s, but already there is the classic Chandler atmosphere: the sleazy, run-down side of the city; the shifty, duplicitous characters; the endless whiskey and cigarettes; the intangible presence of the Great Depression.

From 1939 onwards, Chandler went on to write full-length novels and film scripts. At the centre of all these was the private eye Philip Marlowe, a character very similar to Carmady. On screen, the role was immortalized by Humphrey Bogart.

Chandler's hard-bitten detective won him great popularity with readers and cinema audiences. Chandler remains an important influence on writers of detective stories.

Goldfish

Pre-reading activity

Match the words with the pictures

a 'Get up,' I said.

b 'You're kidding the wrong guy,' Sunset said.

c I blew smoke at the ceiling and looked at her.

d Then Carol was on the floor at my feet, small, deadly, and dead.

e 'May I have them, to remember him with?' said Mrs Sype.

f 'I've got pearls in this – six of them,' said Sype.

g Madder reached over and pulled the phone back.

h There were two guns at the door, one small, one big.

To the teacher

Aim: To familiarize students with the setting and introduce the main characters

Time: 10–20 minutes

Organization: Give one copy of the worksheet to each student or each group of students. Check through the words and explain any unknown meanings. (Alternatively, the students could look up any difficult words in their dictionaries.) Then ask them to match the words with the pictures. When everyone has finished, check the answers. Then, ask students to identify the characters in each picture (by name where possible), and ask for ideas about what might be happening.

Key: 1c, 2g, 3b, 4h, 5a, 6f, 7d, 8e.

Goldfish

While reading activity

Spot the mistakes

These are pages from the diaries of some of the characters in the story. There are three mistakes in each one. Find them and write in the correct words. The first one has been done for you.

I went to see Carmady today. His office is opposite the ~~school~~ *hotel* where I work. I told him about the Leander pearls. I told him there's a reward of $10,000. He's going to try to find them. If he does, I'm going to share the reward money with him and Peeler Mardo. I need the money because my husband's in hospital. When he comes out, I'm going to ...

I agreed to help Kathy. I went to see Mardo to get more information about the pearls, but he was dead. He was lying on the floor. Somebody had burned his hands with an iron. Later I went to see Rush Madder. While we were talking, a girl called Carol Donovan was listening secretly. Madder gave me something strange to drink, and then the girl came in and hit Madder with my sap. They've already left to look for the pearls, but I'm going to ...

Carmady came to see me. I tried to find out what he knew about the pearls, but he didn't know any more than I did. He nearly called the police. I gave him some coffee, and I put something in it to make him sleep for a long time. He hit me a couple of times with his sap, but then Kathy came in and stopped him from doing anything worse. Later, we caught the plane south. Carmady won't be going anywhere for a while. Carol and I are going to ...

To the teacher

Where: At the end of Chapter 3

Aim: To consolidate comprehension of the story before continuing

Time: 15–20 minutes

Organization: Give each student, or each group of students, a copy of the worksheet. There are three factual mistakes in each character's diary entry. Check first that the students recognize the characters. Then ask them to correct the mistakes – the first one has been done for them – and to suggest endings for the incomplete sentences.

Key: Kathy's diary – school: hotel; $10,000: $25,000; hospital: prison; Madder's diary – coffee: whiskey; Kathy came in: Carol came in; south: north; Carmady's diary – floor: bed; hands: feet; hit Madder: hit me.

Goldfish

After reading activity

Snap! or Pelmanism

SET ONE

Carol Donovan	Two	Chinese Moor
Mrs Sype	Westport	$200,000
Something nasty	$12,500	19 years ago
A car key	Wally Sype	Los Angeles
A map	Lutin	Whiskey
Goldfish	Rush Madder	Peeler Mardo
The bathroom	Selling cigars	$25,000
A mail clerk	The Smoke Shop	Kathy Horne
The back of the knee	Mr Wallace	

SET TWO

THIS is the number of pearls that were stolen.	The pearls were hidden in THIS kind of goldfish.	SHE shot Sunset.
Carmady gets THIS at the end of the story	THIS is when the pearls were stolen.	Rush Madder put THIS in Carmandy's whiskey.
Sype changed his name to THIS.	Carmady's office is in THIS city.	Carmady shot Madder HERE.
HE stole the pearls.	HE is a lawyer.	Carmady found THIS in Sunset's pocket.
THIS is Kathy's job.	THIS is the reward money for the pearls.	Carmady locked Carol in HERE.
HE is manager of the insurance company.	THIS is Carmady's favorite drink.	Sunset had THIS in his shoe.
SHE shot Carol Donovan.	HE rented a room in Kathy's house.	Sype had a lot of THESE.
Carmady met Sunset HERE.	SHE used to be a policewoman.	Sype killed HIM during a robbery.
Sype lived HERE.	THIS is how much the Leander pearls cost.	

To the teacher

Aim: To revise key events and facts of the story

Time: 30–40 minutes

Organization: Make a pack of 52 cards by cutting out each of the boxed phrases and sticking them on pieces of card. The pack consists of two sets of 26 cards. The first set has details from the story on the cards (characters, places, numbers and so on), and the second set has clues in the form of complete sentences. The aim is for the students to match up the two sets of cards. The games are best played in groups of three or four students; each group needs a complete pack of 52 cards.

For SNAP! give the players equal numbers of cards, face down. Each player in turn lays one of their cards, face up, on a pile in the centre of the table. If two corresponding cards are put down, one after the other, the player who realizes it first shouts 'Snap!' and can pick up the whole pile of cards in the centre. Play continues until one player holds all the cards and is therefore the winner.

For PELMANISM put all the cards face down on the table, either in parallel rows (this makes the game much easier!) or at different angles to each other. Each player turns over two cards at a time. If the cards are a matching pair, that player keeps both cards, and has another turn. If they do not match, they are turned face down again, and the next person has a turn. Players try to remember where cards are, and the winner is the one with the most pairs of cards at the end of the game.

Go, Lovely Rose and Other Stories

H. E. Bates

Introduction

> *This ungraded summary is for the teacher's use only and should not be given to students.*

The stories

Go, Lovely Rose. It's 3 a.m on a warm summer night and Mr Carteret is waiting for his nineteen-year-old daughter, Susie, to return home. She has been out with twenty-eight-year-old Bill Jordan. Carteret cannot sleep and walks around the garden in his pyjamas, worrying about Susie. Eventually Susie comes home. Carteret hides but Jordan sees him and stops to talk. Carteret is surprised that he is such a polite young man. Before he goes back indoors, Carteret sees a rose. He wants to pick this beautiful flower but decides to leave it. He is now ready to accept that his daughter is independent.

The Daffodil Sky. Bill returns to a town he hasn't visited for many years. He goes to a pub to look for a woman called Cora Whitehead.

Bill used to go out with Cora and often visited her house. One day he decided to buy a farm in the countryside and Cora said that her friend, an older man called Frankie Corbett, could lend them some money to buy it. Bill felt very happy and said that he and Cora could get married.

However, over the next few weeks, Bill grew jealous of Frankie and when Cora became pregnant he was worried that the baby might not be his. One night Bill killed Frankie with a knife. Bill had to go to prison for eighteen years.

Bill now returns to Cora's house, after many years in prison, and meets her grown-up daughter for the first time. He seems to realize that he is her father. His future suddenly looks much brighter.

The Dam. Thirty-eight-year-old George Graham is staying in a hotel in northern Italy where he meets a fifty-year-old widow, Gerda Hauptmann. Gerda is very cold at the beginning but she soon becomes more friendly and seems to be falling in love with George.

Gerda's daughter, twenty-five year old Trudi, comes to join her mother at the hotel. Before Trudi arrives, Gerda paints a very negative picture of her daughter but when George meets her, he finds her very attractive and intelligent.

Gerda now becomes cold and serious again. George, however, is very attracted to Trudi and begins to spend a lot of time with her. She tells George that she blames Gerda for her father's death.

George and Trudi start to have an affair and Gerda is obviously very jealous. One day they all go on a trip to a dam. While George is taking a photo of the two women on top of the high dam, Gerda pushes her daughter and she falls, disappearing into the water.

Background to the stories

The novelist Herbert Ernest Bates was born in 1905 in Northamptonshire, England. After leaving school, Bates went to work as a journalist on a local newspaper, however he soon became interested in writing literature and at the age of twenty he published his first novel *The Two Sisters.*

During the Second World War he served as a pilot and many of his stories of this period are about life during war time. During the 1950's he wrote a series of popular novels about English country life, beginning with *The Darling Buds of May.* These novels, like many other of H. E. Bates' stories, were filmed and turned into a successful T.V. series. Films of his work include *A Month By The Lake* and *A Feast Of July.*

Go, Lovely Rose and Other Stories

Pre-reading activity

Prediction from key words

Put the letters in these words into the correct order.
These words all come from the story The Daffodil Sky.
What do you think the story is about?
What sort of story do you think it might be? (Horror, romance, adventure etc . . .)
Make up your own story using ten of these words.

PLACES	OBJECTS	PEOPLE
rfam.............................	fekin.............................	ybba.............................
onwt.............................	lwofser.............................	nam.............................
ripons.............................	brumelal.............................	mowan.............................
ubp.............................		

VERBS	ADJECTIVES
likl.............................	lufbeuait.............................
siks.............................	ejaolsu.............................
iht.............................	

To the teacher

Aim: To introduce key vocabulary and to encourage students to anticipate the story (*The Daffodil Sky*)
Time: 30 minutes
Organization: Give one copy of the worksheet to each student and ask them to put the letters in the words in the correct order. If any students are not sure about the answers, give some clues to help them. When everyone has finished, go through the answers as a class and check the meaning of any unknown words. Then ask the students to suggest what kind of story might contain these words and what it might be about. Finally, divide the class into small groups and ask them to make up a short story using ten of the words. Some of the stories can be read aloud.
Key: town, prison, pub, knife, flowers, baby, man, woman, umbrella, kill, kiss, hit, beautiful, jealous.

Go, Lovely Rose and Other Stories

After reading activity 1

Spot the mistakes

This is Susie's diary from the next day. There are eleven mistakes in it.
Find them and write in the correct words. The first one has been done for you.

Sunday 25th July

                evening

I went out yesterday ~~lunchtime~~ with Peter Jordan, the man that I recently met on a train. He's really good fun and I haven't had such a great time in ages! He's very interesting and he's got a wonderful motorbike! We went to his father's house and had a delicious meal. After dinner we played tennis until two o'clock in the morning! I enjoyed myself a lot and I can't wait to see them all again. At the end of the evening I walked all the way home on my own in the dark. The weather wasn't very good at all and it was raining. When I got to the house I was very surprised to meet my father. He was looking at the flowers in the garden and he was only wearing shorts and a T-shirt. How strange!

To the teacher

Aim: To help with summarizing and revision of reading (*Go, Lovely Rose*)

Time: 30 minutes

Organization: Give out the extract from Susie's diary, written the day after the events in the story. There are eleven factual mistakes in it and the first one has been done as an example. Give each student, or pair of students, a copy of the summary and ask them to underline the things that are not correct and change them. When everybody has finished, go through the answers as a class and then ask the students to write a diary extract from the point of view of Susie's father.

Key: lunchtime: *evening*; Peter: *Bill*; train: *plane*; motorbike: *car*; father's house: *mother's house*; tennis: *cards*; two o'clock: *three o'clock*; walked home on my own: *came home in Bill's car*; weather not good, raining: *a warm night, no rain*; surprised to meet father: *didn't meet father*; shorts and a T-shirt: *pyjamas*.

Go, Lovely Rose and Other Stories

After reading activity 2

Match words and phrases with each of the three characters

Put these words or phrases next to the most appropriate person.

a sketch book   Johnson   a green coat   sun oil

tall and serious with ice-blue eyes   fifty years old   very attractive   a car

twenty-five years old   Hauptmann   a red dress

room 247   ~~Graham~~   a-yellow dress   afraid of high places

a white swimsuit   thirty-eight years old   a camera   excellent English

not afraid of high places

	WORDS/PHRASES	WHY?
George	*Graham*	*his surname*
Gerda		
Trudi		

To the teacher

Aim: To focus students' attention back on the characters *(The Dam)*

Organization: Give each student or group of students a copy of the chart above. Ask them to identify which word or phrase goes with each character. Go through the answers as a class and then ask students to say how the words or phrases fit into the story.

STAGE 3 — Information Technology

Paul A. Davies

Introduction

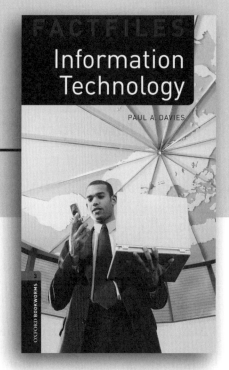

Chapter summary

Chapter 1 (The computer age) looks at how the nineteenth century brought the Industrial Age, with its machines and factories. The twentieth century saw an equally important revolution with the arrival of computing technology.

Chapter 2 (In the beginning) describes how as numbering systems developed, calculations became possible. The abacus was the first mechanical aid to calculation, and in the seventeenth century the first calculating machines were invented.

Chapter 3 (The first computers) looks at the nineteenth century when Charles Babbage started work on two important calculating machines. Ada Lovelace understood Babbage's ideas and wrote the world's first computer program. Progress was made, slowly, over the next hundred years.

Chapter 4 (Alan Turing) shows that during the Second World War there was an urgent need to read coded enemy messages. Turing and others built electronic computers like Colossus, which successfully decoded these messages.

Chapter 5 (The history of the PC) is about the term 'personal computer' and how it was invented to describe a computer that did not need skilled operators. As transistors have continued to become tinier, PCs (dominated by IBM and Apple) have become smaller, cheaper and more powerful.

Chapter 6 (Bill Gates and Microsoft) is about Bill Gates, who was one of the first people to see the future of the PC. His company Microsoft, created operating systems for IBM and Apple, and the development of Windows was a huge success.

Chapter 7 (Humans against computers) looks at computers and activities such as chess which demand calculation and logic. However, no computer has yet passed the 'Turing Test' (demonstrating that it can think like a human).

Chapter 8 (The Internet) tells us that the internet began in the 1970s, but it was the invention of the Web that made it accessible and popular. Many Internet start-up companies failed, but there were spectacular successes too.

Chapter 9 (Power to the people) shows how the Internet is changing lives. A lot more information is now freely available, and people can communicate much more easily.

Chapter 10 (Getting the message) shows that whilst telegraph and telex were both important, e-mails and instant messaging have now become the most popular ways of sending messages.

Chapter 11 (Mobile phones) describes how since the first call in 1973, mobile phones have become smaller, cheaper and better, and there are billions in the world today. They are also used for texting, taking photos and playing games, and many people have their mobiles with them all the time.

Chapter 12 (Computer games) concentrates on computer games. The first were played on big machines in bars and shops. The most successful was Pong, a simple tennis game. Games are now a huge industry and many young people prefer playing them to healthier activities such as sport.

Chapter 13 (I love you (and other viruses)) looks at the first appearance of viruses in the 1980s. Anti-virus software is getting better, but viruses still have the potential to disrupt the computer networks which are essential to modern life.

Chapter 14 (Computer crime) is about criminal activity on the Internet including identity theft, 'phishing' for bank details, the 'Nigerian letter' and the sale of non-existent goods.

Chapter 15 (The future) looks ahead. Transistors and computers are getting smaller, but there is probably a limit to how small they can get. Artificial intelligence and robotics are two areas that currently interest computer scientists, but experience shows that information technology and its uses are likely to change in unpredictable ways.

Information Technology
Pre-reading activity

How much do you know about information technology?

1 Can you match the people and dates to the events?

Who?	What?	When?
Bill Gates	_____ wrote the world's first computer program _____.	in the 1940s
Ada Lovelace	_____ put some songs on the MySpace website _____.	in the 1980s
Alan Turing	_____ invented the Windows computer program _____.	in 2005
Lily Allen	_____ built a computer that could understand secret messages _____.	in 1842

2 Do you think these sentences are true or false? Why?

a There are computer chips in modern washing machines.
b The world's first 'personal computer' cost 1,000 dollars.
c A computer once won a chess match against the best player in the world.
d The program 'I love you' was a popular computer game.
e Every week, about 100 new users join MySpace.

3 Which words do you think will appear in the book? Why?

swimming	war	guitar	mathematics
shoes	memory	sea	pictures
wheels	billionaire	horse	jazz

To the teacher

Aim: To encourage students to predict the content of the book and to introduce key vocabulary
Time: 30 minutes
Organization: Give out the worksheet. Students can first discuss the names, events and dates, and try to match them, guessing if necessary. Then ask students to decide whether sentences a–e are true or false, giving reasons. Finally, check understanding of words in the list and ask students which words they think they will find in the book and why. They can do this as a class or in pairs.

Key 1: First computer program: Ada Lovelace, 1842. Songs on MySpace: Lily Allen, 2005. Windows: Bill Gates, 1980s. Secret messages: Alan Turing, 1940s.
Key 2: a T, b F (it cost 55,000 dollars), c T (against Kasparov in 1997), d F (it was the most successful virus in history), e F (it gets about 500,000 new users every week).
Key 3: Words in the book: war, mathematics, memory, pictures, billionaire, jazz. Words not in the book: swimming, guitar, shoes, sea, wheels, horse.

Information Technology
While reading activity

Order the events

	EVENT	ORDER
a	The search engine Google was invented.	
b	The workers at Bletchley Park built Colossus.	
c	Charles Babbage invented the Difference Engine.	
d	The abacus was invented.	
e	The Microsoft company was started.	
f	The German army started using a code called 'Fish'.	
g	Bill Gates was born.	
h	Blaise Pascal made an Arithmetic Machine.	
i	Alex Tew made the Million Dollar Homepage.	
j	Ada Lovelace wrote the first computer program.	
k	Ed Roberts invented the Altair 8800, a computer that people could put together at home.	
l	The Second World War started.	
m	Bill Gates became a billionaire.	

To the teacher

Where: At the end of chapter 8
Aim: To revise, order and summarize some of the key events so far
Time: 10–20 minutes
Organization: Give out the worksheet to pairs or groups of students and ask them to put the events in the right order, 1–13. (Note that it is not necessary to remember the dates of events, just the sequence.) When they have completed the re-ordering exercise, and it has been checked, ask them to talk about some of the events in more detail. You could also ask students to try to connect some of the sentences using suitable linking words or phrases.
Key: 1d, 2h, 3c, 4j, 5l, 6f, 7b, 8g, 9k, 10e, 11m, 12a, 13i.

Information Technology
After reading activity

Cross word

```
        [1]
    [2]
[3]
  [4]
      [5]
  [6]
      [7]
    [8]
  [9]
[10]
    [11]
```

1 The robot Miss Rong Cheng can speak this language.
2 A program that helps people find information on the Web.
3 This computer was very good at playing chess.
4 This website has information on millions of subjects.
5 A diary on the Internet that everyone can read.
6 You can see Charles Babbage's Difference Engine in the _____ Museum in London.
7 A simple computer game (like tennis) that was very popular in the 1970s.
8 When criminals try to get information from people by sending dishonest emails.
9 The Bill and Melinda Gates _____ has given a lot of money to schools, hospitals and libraries.
10 No computer has ever passed the _____ Test, because computers cannot think like humans.
11 If a text message says 'CU L8R', it means '____ ____ later.'

To the teacher

Aim: To revise and discuss some of the main characters, themes and events

Time: 20–30 minutes

Organization: Give each student, or group of students, a copy of the word grid. Ask the students to read the clues, write in the eleven words and find the hidden words running down the centre. Go through the answers as a class and see how much the students can remember, and what they think, about some of the topics mentioned. For example: How have mobile phones changed people's lives? What jobs do you think robots might do in the future? Will computers ever be able to think and have emotions like people? Do young people spend too long playing computer games?

Key: 1 Mandarin, 2 Google, 3 Deep Blue, 4 Wikipedia, 5 Blog, 6 Science, 7 Pong, 8 Phishing, 9 Foundation, 10 Turing, 11 See you. Hidden words: mobile phone.

Justice

Tim Vicary

Introduction

The story

When a bomb explodes in the Queen's coach at the opening of Parliament, the driver, Alan Cole, is one of those badly injured. His daughter Jane sees the explosion, for which a group of Irish terrorists later claim responsibility. In hospital, Alan tells Jane about his girlfriend Anna who visited the horses with him the night before the bombing. Jane goes to Anna's house with a letter from her father, but a neighbour tells her that Anna has moved out – with her boyfriend Kev. Jane feels very sorry for her father.

When Jane returns to her flat, she is surprised by a man and a woman, who tie her up. Jane realizes that the woman is Anna, her father's friend, and that she has seen her before – outside Parliament when the bomb exploded. Anna rings Alan in hospital and threatens to kill Jane if he tells the police about Anna. Frightened, Alan tells the police that he was alone when he visited the horses the evening before the bomb, but later he tells the police the truth, and they begin to search for Jane.

Anna and Kev move Jane from her flat to a house, where they tie her to a bed, but Jane manages to cut herself free. While Anna is out of the house, Kev brings Jane some coffee, and she attacks him. There is a desperate struggle and Kev's gun goes off, killing him. Jane escapes from the house and goes to an underground station, but Anna sees her and follows her. Jane runs into a tunnel to hide, but Anna finds her, and the two women fight beside the train line. Finally Jane pushes Anna away and she falls under a train. When Jane comes out of the tunnel, her father is there with the police. Now Anna and Kev, who caused five deaths, are themselves dead. 'There is some justice,' says Jane. She and her father comfort each other.

Background to the story

The threat of terrorist violence has overshadowed British–Irish relations for many years. Since the late 1960s there have been numerous periods of intense terrorist activity, interspersed with quieter periods or ceasefires. The principal group involved in terrorist activity against targets in England has been the IRA (Irish Republican Army), an Irish military organization which seeks to unite Northern Ireland with the Republic of Ireland as a single independent state.

Terrorist attacks have focused on a variety of targets. Army targets were popular at first; later, terrorists chose targets which would bring maximum publicity (e.g. the bombing of the luxury department store Harrods), or maximum disruption (e.g. the bombing of London's docklands in 1996, or in more recent times threats to blow up bridges on major motorways). The bombing of the Queen's coach outside the Houses of Parliament described in the book could be expected to bring both publicity and disruption on a grand scale.

Before reading

Here are some ways to help your students approach the story:

1 Give students the title of the book and show them the picture on the cover. Ask them to try and guess what kind of the story it is.

2 Give students a copy of the text on the back cover of the book, and of the story introduction on the first page. When they have read the texts, ask them a few questions about the story, or use the Before Reading Activities in the back of each Bookworm.

3 Use the pre-reading activity in this worksheet.

4 If there is a recording of this title, play the first few pages and stop at an interesting point.

Justice
Pre-reading activity

Match the words with the pictures

☐ **a** The woman shook her camera angrily.

☐ **b** 'Get this horse off me!'

☐ **c** Jane stroked her father's hand softly.

☐ **d** 'It's a bit difficult, Janie. Anna has a husband.'

☐ **e** 'They've gone; there's no use waiting.'

☐ **f** Who were these people? What did they want with her?

☐ **g** They had gone to the Mews to look at the horses.

To the teacher

Aim: To familiarize students with the setting and characters

Time: 5–10 minutes

Organization: Give a copy of the worksheet to each student or pair of students. Ask them to match the words with the pictures. When they have done this, ask them the following questions:

1 Where does this story happen?
2 Can they identify in the pictures:
a the father
b the daughter
c the father's girlfriend
d the neighbour
Key: 1b, 2e, 3f, 4c, 5a, 6g, 7d.

Justice
While reading activity

Jane's journey

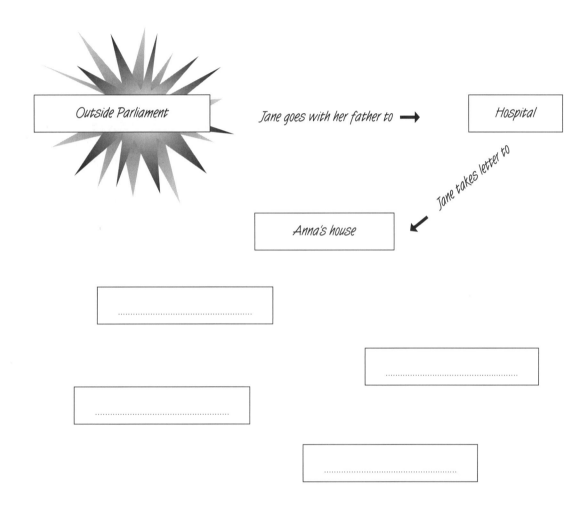

Other locations: Jane's flat, an underground station, Anna and Kev's house, a tunnel.

To the teacher

Where: At the text break * * * on page 17
Aim: To speculate about the development of the plot
Time: 10–15 minutes
Organization: Give students a copy of the worksheet showing the beginning of Jane's 'journey' through the book. They may work individually, in pairs or in groups. Tell them that the other locations listed are those which Jane goes to in the course of the book, though not necessarily in the order given. Ask them to continue the journey, adding the other locations

in the order that they think they might occur. They should write in any other significant details that they think might take place (for example, who goes with Jane? what happens?)
When they have finished, they can compare their diagrams with other students and see whether they have produced similar diagrams or not. As they continue to read the story, they will discover how accurately or not they have predicted the outcome.

Justice
After reading activity

'Justice' in Hollywood

Your group is responsible for producing a film of Justice.
Discuss and complete the sections below.

ACTORS

Choose actors from those you know for the
characters from the book.

Alan ....

Jane ....

Anna ....

Kev ....

FILM DIRECTOR

Think of films you know and choose a
film director who would be good for
your film. ....

FILM TITLE

Choose two titles.

1 A sentence from
   the book *Justice* ....

2 Your own idea ....

MUSIC

Choose an artist,
group or composer
for the film. ....

PRODUCT

Choose a product to
be sold with the film. ....

To the teacher

Aim: To reassess plot and theme

Time: 15–20 minutes

Organization: Divide the class into small groups and
give out the worksheets. Each group is responsible
for producing a film of 'Justice'; their task is to
search through the world of film and come up with
names for the different sections on the worksheet.

Once each group has made its choices, they can
reveal them to the class in discussion or by displaying
their list of chosen actors etc. . . They should be
prepared to explain and justify their choices. Further
discussion may follow concerning the best choices,
the most appropriate product etc.

Kidnapped

Robert Louis Stevenson

Introduction

> *This ungraded summary is for the teacher's use only and should not be given to students.*

Kidnapped

ROBERT LOUIS STEVENSON

The story

It is the year 1751, in Scotland. At the age of seventeen, after the death of both his parents, David Balfour leaves his home village. He is on his way to find his uncle Ebenezer, who he has never met. He finds his uncle, clearly a rich man, but living in a miserly way in a large half-finished house, near Edinburgh. He is clearly afraid of David – indeed he tries to kill him – and it becomes apparent that he thinks David is after his money and his house. And as it appears that Ebenezer is David's father's *younger* brother it would seem that David does have a claim.

To get rid of David, Ebenezer arranges for a sea captain to kidnap him aboard his ship. The idea is to take David as a prisoner to America, and sell him there as a slave.

While sailing around the north of Scotland in a fog, the ship hits a smaller boat. They save one of the passengers, Alan Breck, but all the others are drowned. Alan Breck is a Highlander – an opponent of the English King George, and he offers to pay the captain to put him down on the north-west coast of Scotland where he will be among friends. But David discovers that the captain is secretly planning to kill Breck and steal his money. He tells Breck, and together they fight the crew of the ship – and win. Shortly after this, however, the ship is wrecked – off the island of Mull – near the west coast of Scotland.

David is separated from the crew of the ship – and from Alan Breck – by the shipwreck. He makes his way across Mull, where he discovers that the Highlanders are assembling again to fight King George's soldiers. As a Lowlander, David is a supporter of King George, but he was very impressed with Alan Breck, and he begins to feel some sympathy for the Highlanders. Eventually he meets up with Alan Breck again. Although the two men are on different sides, they both find themselves wrongly accused of murder, and decide to travel together across Scotland. David hopes to find a lawyer who can help him reclaim his inheritance.

They have a number of dangerous adventures on their journey, and David is also seriously ill. However, they eventually reach Queensferry, near Edinburgh, where David is able to contact a lawyer. Together with Alan Breck they are able to recover David's fortune from his uncle. Once this is done, it is dangerous for Alan to remain in Scotland, and David arranges for him to escape to France and safety.

Background to the story

The story is set in the aftermath of the 1745 uprising in Scotland. Scotland and England had had the same king for more than a hundred years, but many Highland Scots contested the legitimacy of the Protestant King George and preferred the Catholic Prince Charles Stuart ('Bonnie Prince Charlie'), who came from the Scottish royal family. The uprising of Charles Stuart's Highland supporters in 1745, initially successful, was cruelly suppressed by both the English and the Scottish supporters of King George. Charles Stuart and his principal supporters fled to France. Thus the Scottish Highlands that the two friends cross in the story has been the site of a bloody war, and is effectively under the control of an occupying army. The two main protagonists, of course, come from opposite sides in the conflict – but their mutual respect enables them to maintain their friendship.

Kidnapped

Pre-reading activity

Who's who?

1 *Match the words with the pictures.*

a 'If you can take me to France, I'll pay you well,' said Alan Breck.

b I shut the door behind me for the last time.

c 'Give me Alexander's letter!' cried Ebenezer.

d 'Goodbye,' I said, and took his hand.

e We all three stood looking down at Mr Shaun.

f 'Do you want us to kill or keep the lad?' said Alan.

g We fell down in the heather, and lay without moving.

h I lifted my pistol and shot at them.

2 *Now complete the sentences.*

a David Balfour is the man who tells the story. He has a friend called ....

b .... gets into danger with his friend David.

c .... is an old man, and David's uncle.

d .... is a sailor who drinks too much.

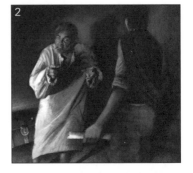

To the teacher

Aim: To familiarize the students with the setting and characters.

Time: 10–15 minutes

Organization: Give one copy of the worksheet to each student or group of students. Ask them to

match the words with the pictures. From the results of this matching activity they should be able to write in the names of the characters in Activity 2.

Key: Activity 1: 1b, 2c, 3e, 4a, 5h, 6g, 7f, 8d.

Activity 2: a Alan (Breck), b Alan (Breck), c Ebenezer, d Mr Shaun.

Kidnapped
While reading activity

What will happen next?

Alan
Will help David escape from the Campbells.
Will die.
Will help David get his money from his uncle.
Will go back to France.
Will help Ebenezer kill David.
(something else)

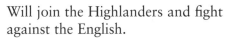

David
Will go to prison for helping with the murder of Campbell.
Will run away with Alan Breck.
Will join the Highlanders and fight against the English.
Will get his money from his uncle.
Will kill his uncle.
Will take Alan prisoner and give him to the Campbells.
(something else)

Uncle Ebenezer
Will die.
Will give David his money.
Will pay someone to kill David.
Will disappear with all the money.
(something else)

To the teacher

Where: At the end of Chapter 3
Aim: To encourage predictions on the development of the story and its characters
Time: 15–20 minutes
Organization: Give one copy of the worksheet to each student or group of students. Ask the students to make their predictions on what will happen to each of the characters. They may want to retain their predictions to compare with what actually happens in the story.

Kidnapped

After reading activity

Order the events

	EVENT	ORDER
a	Cluny returns David's money to him.	
b	The boatmen tell David he can leave Earraid when the tide is low.	
c	Hoseason kidnaps David.	
d	Somebody shoots Campbell and David and Alan meet again.	*10*
e	David tells his story to Mr Rankeillor.	
f	Alan Breck comes on to the ship.	
g	David's mother and father die.	*1*
h	Alan talks to Ebenezer about the kidnapping.	
i	David and Alan hide all day on a rock.	
j	David and Alan fight the sailors.	
k	Alan and David say goodbye.	
l	Alan and David reach the Lowlands.	
m	David meets his uncle Ebenezer.	
n	Ebenezer agrees to pay David.	
o	Mr Shuan kills Ransome.	
p	Rankeillor, Torrance and David hide below the steps at Ebenezer's house.	
q	David goes into Queensferry and finds Mr Rankeillor.	
r	David falls ill and Alan loses all David's money at cards.	
s	David discovers that Ebenezer is the younger brother.	
t	The ship hits a rock and David swims to Earraid.	

To the teacher

Aim: To order, revise, remember what has been read, summarize

Time: 10–20 minutes

Organization: Give one copy of the worksheet to each student or group of students. Ask them to try and remember the order in which events happened, without looking at the book. Once they have agreed an order, they may wish to go back and check that they have remembered correctly by referring to the book.

Key: 1g, 2m, 3s, 4c, 5o, 6f, 7j, 8t, 9b, 10d, 11i, 12r, 13a, 14l, 15q, 16e, 17p, 18h, 19n, 20k.

The Last Sherlock Holmes Story

Michael Dibdin

Introduction

> This ungraded summary is for the teacher's use only and should not be given to students.

The Last Sherlock Holmes Story

MICHAEL DIBDIN

OXFORD BOOKWORMS

The story

The story is found in a box left by Dr Watson, Holmes's friend, when it is opened fifty years after Watson's death. After ten years as a detective, Holmes is famous but bored. He begins taking cocaine to provide excitement in his life. Then the police ask for his help in catching Jack the Ripper – a criminal who kills and mutilates women. Holmes laughs at first, then agrees to help. That night two women die, but although Holmes and the police pursue the murderer, he escapes.

A few weeks later Holmes tells Watson that the Ripper is in fact a super-intelligent criminal called Professor Moriarty. One night, Holmes sends Watson for help while he follows Moriarty, but Watson secretly follows him, and sees him meet a woman. He falls asleep while waiting for Holmes. When he wakes, he discovers to his horror that the woman is dead – and Holmes is cutting her up.

Holmes leaves the country, supposedly in pursuit of Moriarty. Watson, shocked and fearful, moves out of London. Holmes claims that Moriarty has now gone, and travels further, working on other cases. When he returns he seems calmer, and stops using drugs. He and Watson become friends again.

After a couple of years, however, the murderer strikes again. One day Holmes arrives to see Watson. He is anxious and excited, having discovered that Moriarty is not dead. Watson drugs Holmes and searches his rooms and then the house opposite. There he finds papers about the murders and jars containing pieces of dead bodies. Holmes sets off again after Moriarty, and Watson goes with him, drugging himself so he can watch Holmes. Finally, after a wild run of several days, Watson confronts Holmes at the Reichenbach Falls. The deluded Holmes tries to kill Watson, thinking he is Moriarty, but in a last lucid moment realizes that he himself is endangering his friend, and he jumps to his death.

Background to the story

In this story the author cleverly brings together two celebrated British personalities, one fictitious, one widely publicized but never positively identified. The fictitious character, Sherlock Holmes, is one of the most famous detectives in literature. He first appeared in Sir Arthur Conan Doyle's *A Study In Scarlet* in 1887, and went on to appear in many more stories, dazzling readers with his energy, his eccentricities and his astonishing mental powers. The second character, Jack the Ripper, is the name given to an unidentified murderer who killed and mutilated six prostitutes in the East End of London in 1888. In spite of great public uproar and extensive investigation, the murderer was never found or even identified. Speculation over his identity continues to this day. The author merges detective and murderer into a single character, always one step ahead of the police, but always on the borderline between brilliance and insanity.

Before reading

Here are some ways to help your students approach the story:

1   Give students the title of the book and show them the picture on the cover. Ask them to try and guess what kind of the story it is.

2   Give students a copy of the text on the back cover of the book, and of the story introduction on the first page. When they have read the texts, ask them a few questions about the story, or use the Before Reading Activities in the back of each Bookworm.

3   Use the pre-reading activity in this worksheet.

4   If there is a recording of this title, play the first few pages and stop at an interesting point.

The Last Sherlock Homes Story
Pre-reading activity

Wicked words / Detectives and criminals

Wicked words
Write down as many detective and crime words as you can. The more unusual words you have, the more points your team will get!

....
....
....
....
....
....

What do you know?
Write down any information you know about Sherlock Holmes and Jack the Ripper.

....
....
....
....
....
....
....

Detectives and Criminals

Group A
How are detectives and criminals similar? Write down as many answers as you can.

....
....
....
....
....
....
....

Group B
How are detectives and criminals different? Write down as many answers as you can.

....
....
....
....
....
....
....

To the teacher

Aim: To check on and pool relevant vocabulary items (wicked words)/To draw out existing knowledge and focus on a major theme of the story (detectives and criminals).

Time: 5–10 minutes (Wicked words)/10–15 minutes (Detectives and Criminals)

Organization: Copy the worksheet and cut it up at the appropriate points. Give out the first half of the worksheet and divide students into small groups and ask them to do the first task. After a few minutes tell the groups to stop. Ask each group in turn to give you the words they have found, and list them on the board. Each group gets a point for any word they have found that is on no other group's list. Students can then add the new words to their list; they may be useful in the activity that follows.

For the second task, allow five minutes for students to answer What do you know? on their worksheet. Then pool the information from the class onto the board. If necessary, tell students that they are a celebrated detective and a celebrated murderer from late nineteenth century England.

For Detectives and Criminals divide the class into A and B groups and give out the A and B questions. The As write down as many answers as they can to their question. The Bs do the same with theirs. Allow five minutes, then ask the groups to report back to the class.

The Last Sherlock Holmes Story
While reading activity

Chapter headings

Alternative heading for *Introduction*:

F R I E N D S

    F uture readers will see this
    R ubbish – ACD's book
    I n love with Mary
    E vil is the enemy
    N o success with A Study in Scarlet
    D r Watson feels hurt
    S herlock still has cocaine

Alternative heading for *The first murders*:

....
....
....
....
....
....
....
....

Alternative heading for *Professor Moriarty*:

....
....
....
....
....
....
....
....
....
....
....
....

Alternative heading for *Jack the Ripper kills again*:

....
....
....
....
....
....
....
....
....
....

To the teacher

Where: At the end of Chapter 3
Aim: To make subjective mini-summaries through selection of key points and impressions
Time: 20 minutes
Organization: Give out the worksheet and ask students in groups to come up with an alternative chapter heading for Chapters 1, 2, and 3 – preferably a heading of one or two words. Then, as in the example for the *Introduction*, they write it vertically down the page. They then write associated ideas horizontally alongside the chosen heading, the first letter of each idea being part of the vertical wording.

The Last Sherlock Holmes Story

After reading activity

Similarities and differences

| | DIFFERENCES | | SIMILARITIES |
	Holmes	Watson	
Character	brilliant easily bored	less bright content	interested in crime
Experience	single detective	married doctor	live in London

To the teacher

Aim: To analyse and compare character

Time: 20–30 minutes

Organization: Give students a copy of the worksheet. Ask them to work in pairs or small groups to find as many similarities and differences between the two major characters as they can, referring to the book where necessary, and enter them on the worksheet. At the end of the allotted time, students could either report verbally to the class or display their work. Students may also want to discuss their findings or ask other groups to justify what they have written, especially in the case of more original conclusions.

The Long White Cloud: Stories from New Zealand

Retold by Christine Lindop

Introduction

The stories

The Long White Cloud is a collection of four stories from New Zealand.

After the Earthquake is set in New Zealand more than a century ago. The Blakiston family live on a farm near a small town, and know everybody in the community. Walter is six years old, and his mother is constantly warning him not to ask too many questions. One night an earthquake causes some damage to their property and Walter wishes he could see an earthquake happening. He goes shopping with his mother the next day, and the store keeper tells them that Mrs Duncaster died of shock after the earthquake. Walter goes with his mother to visit Miss Duncaster, who lived with her mother and is now alone. Walter notices a farmer's horse tied to the verandah but when he asks Miss Duncaster about the horse she becomes angry with him. Later, Walter asks his father about the horse, and his father admits that Walter saw the horse but he tells Walter that he must not talk about it.

Gathering of the Whakapapa tells the story of a Māori village whose written genealogy has been destroyed in a fire. Nani Tama, the old man who has been trained in the village genealogy, is grief-stricken by this loss. He works for about two years, chanting the names from memory while one of his grandchildren writes down the names. In spite of his ill-health, he insists on travelling to visit another old man who will remember the last missing names from the genealogy. On his return home, Nani Tama gives the completed whakapapa to the village, and is then ready to die.

A Kind of Longing tells the story of Roy, a young man who enjoys fishing and riding his motorbike. His friend was killed in a plane crash, and this loss makes him feel lonely. The story describes Roy's journey home after a fishing trip. The back tyre bursts, and he has to leave his bike at a farm. He begins the long walk home, hoping for a lift from a passing vehicle. But no one stops to give him a lift until at last a bike stops for

him. Roy discovers that the girl rider knows about both bikes and fishing, and that her brother was killed in an accident, and he feels a strong bond with her. On their way home they have an accident, caused by a car on the wrong side of the road, but they survive to face the future together.

The Silk is the story of an elderly couple facing the death of the husband. Mr Blackie brought some beautiful silk from China for his wife's wedding present, and Mrs Blackie suggests she uses the silk to make laying-out pyjamas for her husband. Mr Blackie watches as his wife sews the pyjamas and tries them on with delight when they are finished. He dies the next day and Mrs Blackie is comforted when she sees something in the pictures on the silk which she has never noticed before: the figure of a man who seems to be waving at her, or beckoning her to join him.

STAGE 3

The Long White Cloud: Stories from New Zealand

Pre-reading activity

Picture match

Match the pictures with the words and the story titles

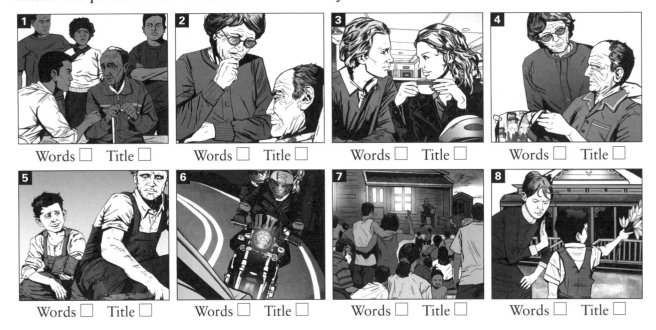

Words ☐ Title ☐   Words ☐ Title ☐   Words ☐ Title ☐   Words ☐ Title ☐

Words ☐ Title ☐   Words ☐ Title ☐   Words ☐ Title ☐   Words ☐ Title ☐

Words

a Smiling, he lifted up the whakapapa and offered it to the village.

b Miss Duncaster bent down and hit him on the arm with her open hand.

c He crossed his arms. 'You did a really good job, Amy. Think I'll keep them on for a bit.'

d The lights of the car were right in front of them. They had nowhere to go.

e Mr Blakiston, with Walter's help, began to clear the bricks from the roof of the wash-house.

f Gently she picked up the blue silk and let it fall in a river over his fingers.

g It was a shock to see him; he was so thin and his skin seemed so grey.

h In the coffee shop he saw her face for the first time, and he felt that kind of longing from way back.

Story Titles (use each title twice)

i After the Earthquake

j Gathering of the Whakapapa

k A Kind of Longing

l The Silk

To the teacher

Aim: To encourage students to predict the setting and themes of the four stories

Time: 30 minutes

Organization: Put the students into pairs after they have read the cover and the introduction. Give one copy of the worksheet to each pair. Ask them to discuss and predict which story belongs to which picture, and then add the words to the pictures. They may need to use a dictionary to check some of the more unusual words. Check the answers with the whole class. The important thing is to begin thinking about the stories, not the accuracy of the answers.

Key: 1aj, 2bi, 3cl, 4dk, 5ei, 6fl, 7gj, 8hk

The Long White Cloud: Stories from New Zealand

While reading activity

Getting it right

Correct as many mistakes as possible.

> *walked*
> I ~~rode~~ the Norton to a house up the road, and left it in one of the farm buildings. I
>
> started to run, but no one stopped to give me a ride. I had walked for miles when I
>
> heard my favourite sound. It was a small modern bike, and the rider was a girl, Kay.
>
> She knows about cars and she knows about fishing. She is the girl I have longed for
>
> all my life! We stopped for tea at the next town, and talked – about her sister who
>
> was killed, and about my friend. We rode again, and suddenly there was a bike on
>
> the wrong side of the road, right behind us. We were off the road, crashing down the
>
> river, into the thick water of the ditch. I pulled myself along, until I found Kay. She
>
> began to cry, and I put my gloves round her.

To the teacher

Where: At the end of A Kind of Longing
Aim: To help with summarizing and revision of A Kind of Longing
Time: 30 minutes
Organization: Give out the extract from Roy's diary, written after the accident. There are eleven factual mistakes in it and the first one has been corrected as an example. Ask the students, or pairs of students, to change the mistakes. When everybody has finished, go through the answers as a class and then ask the students to write a diary extract from Kay's point of view.

Key: run: walk; small: big; cars: bikes; tea: coffee; sister: brother; bike: car; behind: in front of; river: bank; thick: icy; gloves: arms

The Long White Cloud: Stories from New Zealand

After reading activity

Crossword

Words across

1 a strong feeling of wanting something
2 how fast something is moving
3 one of the soft light parts that cover a bird's body
4 to let out a long deep breath to show you are sad, tired, etc.
5 of a pale yellowish-white colour

Words down

6 something sticky that is used for joining things together
7 a long channel at the side of a road that takes away water
8 the ability to remember things
9 a kind of fine smooth cloth that is made from the threads of an insect
10 a man (*informal*)

To the teacher

Aim: To consolidate vocabulary

Time: 20 minutes

Organization: Give one copy of the word search to each student or divide students into pairs. If they are in pairs, they can take it in turns to guess the words from the clues. All the words are from the glossary at the back of the book. When the activity has been completed, go through the words and deal with any difficulties over meaning.

Key: 1 longing, 2 speed, 3 feather, 4 sigh, 5 creamy, 6 glue, 7 ditch, 8 memory, 9 silk, 10 guy

STAGE 3

Love Story

Erich Segal

Introduction

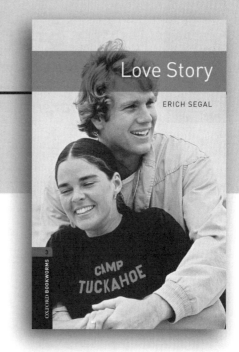

The story

Oliver Barrett, who is studying at Harvard University, meets a girl called Jenny Cavilleri, who is studying at Radcliffe University. They are very different people, in terms of background, character and interests. Oliver's father is a wealthy banker, and Jenny's is a hard-working baker. Oliver's great interest is sport, and Jenny's is music. Their attitudes to their families are different, too. Jenny is very close to her father, and calls him by his first name, while Oliver always seems annoyed with his father, and cannot communicate with him.

Despite these differences, Oliver and Jenny fall in love, and decide to marry after their graduation. Oliver's father thinks his son is getting married too young, and refuses to allow him any more money. Oliver has three years of law school ahead of him before he can practise as a lawyer, and is too proud to plead with his father, so Jenny gives up her music scholarship in Paris and works as a teacher to support Oliver. They are very poor, but happy. Jenny tries hard to bring Oliver and his father together, but without success. Finally, Oliver finishes at law school, with excellent results, and is immediately offered a well-paid job with a large company in New York. Now they are comfortably off, and can look forward to having a baby.

But nothing happens, and when they go to consult a doctor, he tells Oliver that Jenny is dying of a serious blood disease. Oliver is horrified and tries to keep it a secret from Jenny, but she soon discovers the truth. A month later Jenny goes into hospital. Oliver has to borrow a lot of money from his father to pay the medical bills, but he still cannot bring himself to talk properly to his father, or tell him about Jenny. She dies in Oliver's arms. Oliver's father hears about her illness, and comes to offer help. For the first time, Oliver breaks down, and accepts his father's love and support.

Background to the story

The author, Erich Segal, was born in 1937. *Love Story*, published in 1970, was his first novel. It became an international bestseller and a very popular film.

The story is set in the USA, in the late 1960s, when the British pop group The Beatles were at the height of their popularity. Harvard is one of the most respected and prestigious universities in North America, and is on the East coast of the United States. A classic career path for an American lawyer would be to graduate from Harvard University, then study for three more years at Harvard Law School, in order to take the final qualifying legal exams, as Oliver does in the story. Traditional universities, like Harvard and Yale, often consider sporting ability to be almost as important as intellectual achievement, and a high sporting profile may even help a graduate to gain employment.

Before reading

Here are some ways to help your students approach the story:

1   Give students the title of the book and show them the picture on the cover. Ask them to try and guess what kind of the story it is.

2   Give students a copy of the text on the back cover of the book, and of the story introduction on the first page. When they have read the texts, ask them a few questions about the story, or use the Before Reading Activities in the back of each Bookworm.

3   Use the pre-reading activity in this worksheet.

4   If there is a recording of this title, play the first few pages and stop at an interesting point.

Love Story
Pre-reading activity

Word search

S	C	H	O	L	A	R	S	H	I	P	H
C	W	O	Z	A	F	P	O	O	R	I	U
O	D	C	Q	W	A	P	A	S	T	A	S
R	Y	K	E	Y	T	J	Q	P	V	N	B
E	I	E	X	E	H	F	X	I	Z	O	A
X	N	Y	A	R	E	L	A	T	I	O	N
W	G	J	M	A	R	R	I	A	G	E	D
K	I	S	S	G	I	R	L	L	O	V	E

Write your answers here.

....

....

Write sentences using two or more of these words each time.

....

....

....

....

....

....

....

....

To the teacher

Aim: To introduce students to key vocabulary
Time: 15–20 minutes
Organization: Give one copy of the word search to each student or put the word search on an overhead projector. Give the students ten minutes to find as many words as possible. Go through words they have identified and help them with the meanings of

any difficult words. Ask students to suggest what kind of story might include these words, and then ask them to make sentences using two or more of these words each time.
Key: scholarship, poor, pasta, key, relation, marriage, kiss, girl, love, score, dying, hockey, exam, lawyer, father, hospital, piano, husband.

Love Story

After reading activity 1

Order the events

	EVENT	ORDER
a	Oliver's father becomes Head of the Peace Corps.	
b	Oliver and Jenny get married.	
c	Oliver gets angry, and Jenny walks out.	
d	They discover that Jenny is dying.	
e	Jenny watches Oliver play in the Dartmouth match.	
f	Jenny asks Oliver to hold her as she dies.	
g	Oliver and Jenny make love for the first time.	
h	Oliver and Jenny move to New York.	
i	Oliver goes to borrow a book from the Radcliffe library.	
j	Oliver's mother sends a birthday party invitation.	
k	Oliver rings Jenny to tell her he's in love with her.	
l	Oliver's father takes him out to dinner.	
m	Oliver takes Jenny to meet his parents.	
n	Oliver takes Jenny for coffee.	
o	Jenny takes Oliver to meet her father.	
p	Oliver's great-grandfather gives Barrett Hall to Harvard University.	
q	Oliver cries in his father's arms.	
r	Phil moves into the New York flat.	

Snap! or Pelmanism

SET ONE

Twenty-five	Scoring goals	Ray Stratton
Mozart, Bach and the-Beatles	The piano	Paris
The Radcliffe library,	Old Stonyface	Italian cakes
Glasses	Twelve stitches	Bozo
Five million	A non-conversation	Joans and Marsh
Italy	The Olympic Games	Just be natural
Harvard University	Phil	Five thousand dollars
Preppie	MG sports car	Cleaning the flat
	The last word	Crying

To the teacher

Aim: To revise events and key facts of the narrative

Time: 30–40 minutes

Organization: Make a pack of fifty-two cards by cutting out and sticking each of the words and sentences on a piece of card. The pack consists of two sets of twenty-six cards. The first set has characters, actions or objects on the cards, and the second set has complete sentences with information from the story. The aim is for students to match up the two sets of cards. The games are best played in groups of three or four students: each group needs a complete pack of fifty-two cards.

For SNAP! give the players equal numbers of cards, face down. Each player in turn lays one of their cards, face up, on a pile in the centre of the-table. If two corresponding cards are put down, one after the other, the player who realizes it first shouts 'Snap!' and can pick up the whole pile of cards in the centre. Play continues until one player holds all the cards and is therefore the winner.

For PELMANISM put all the cards face down on the table, either in parallel rows (this makes it much easier!) or at different angles to each other. Each player turns over two cards at a time. If the cards are a matching pair, that player keeps both cards, and has another turn. If they do not match, they are turned over again, and the next person has a turn. Players try to remember where cards are, and the winner is the one with the most pairs of cards at the end of the game.

Love Story
After reading activity 2

Snap! or Pelmanism

SET TWO

Oliver and Jenny first meet HERE.

Jenny sometimes wears THESE.

Oliver's father was chosen to play in THESE.

Jenny's father comes from HERE.

Oliver studies HERE.

Jenny plays THIS instrument.

Oliver sometimes thinks of his father like THIS.

Jenny calls her father THIS.

Oliver has to have THESE in his face after an ice hockey match.

THIS is Oliver's car.

Jenny loves having THIS.

HE is a good friend of Oliver's.

Jenny wins a scholarship to study music HERE.

Jenny dies at THIS age.

Jenny loves THIS type of music.

Harvard had THIS number of books.

Jenny sometimes calls Oliver THIS.

THIS is what Oliver likes doing!

THIS is what Oliver thinks talking to his father is like.

Oliver eats THESE on his first visit to Jenny's father.

Oliver wants to call his son this.

Oliver accepts a highly-paid job with THIS company.

THIS is what the doctor tells Oliver to do.

Oliver borrows THIS from his father.

Phil does THIS, again and again.

Oliver says strong men don't do THIS.

Martin Luther King

Alan C. Mclean

Introduction

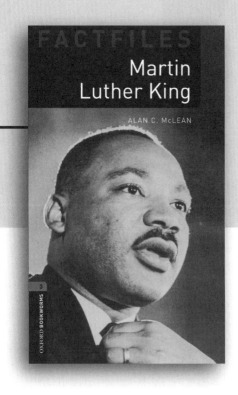

Chapter summary

Chapter 1 (The man from Alabama) looks at 1963 when Martin Luther King led a march of more than quarter of a million people to Washington to demand equal rights for black Americans. Yet five years later, he was murdered. Why was this man so loved and so hated?

Chapter 2 (Growing up in the south) shows that although he came from a middle-class family (his father was a minister of the church), Martin experienced racism from an early age.

Chapter 3 (Slavery and the South) describes how in 1929, most black Americans lived in the South and were the descendants of slaves brought over from Africa. Although the slave trade was abolished in 1808, whites in the South demanded the right to keep slaves.

Chapter 4 (War in America – and after) describes a bloody war between the North and the South which ended slavery in the South. Now they were free, many blacks moved to work in the North. Blacks began to play a more prominent part in American life.

Chapter 5 (Learning) looks at Martin Luther King as a student who was much influenced by the non-violent teachings of Gandhi. In 1954 he became a minister in Montgomery, Alabama.

Chapter 6 (The Montgomery bus boycott) is about Rosa Parks who was arrested for refusing to give up her seat to a white man on a Montgomery bus. Martin Luther King organised a boycott of the city's buses due to this. The boycott lasted a year but it ended segregation in Montgomery.

Chapter 7 (Big trouble in Little Rock) shows how segregation in schools had ended but many Southern states refused to obey the law. When nine black students tried to enter the Little Rock High School, white protesters rioted and the army had to be called in to stop the riots.

Chapter 8 (A new start?) describes how sit-ins in whites-only restaurants in the South succeeded in ending segregation there. Martin Luther King was imprisoned for his part in the protests.

Chapter 9 (From Birmingham to Washington) looks at police violence against peaceful protesters in Alabama and how it shocked shocked the nation. In August 1963 Martin Luther King made a famous speech to a huge crowd in Washington.

Chapter 10 ('This country is sick!') moves to a year later when Martin Luther King won the Nobel Peace Prize, but continued his valuable work. He campaigned to register more black Americans to vote.

Chapter 11 ('I'm black and I'm proud!') shows how many young blacks were impatient with Martin Luther King's policy of non-violence. The Black Panthers and Malcolm X thought that only the use of violence would bring about real change.

Chapter 12 ('Black and white, unite and fight!') is about when Martin Luther King widened the scope of his activities. He spoke out against poverty in America and protested against the Vietnam War. Some black leaders were uneasy about this change of direction.

Chapter 13 (Death in Memphis) looks at 1968 when Martin Luther King went to Memphis to support striking workers. He made a speech in which he urged people to carry on his work even after his death. The next day he was shot dead.

Chapter 14 (Still dreaming) describes how Martin Luther King's death shocked the whole country. People knew they had lost an inspirational leader. Thousands came to his funeral. In 1983 his birthday became a national holiday. Today his work is continued by the Martin Luther King Center.

Background

The South has always been the poorest part of the USA. In the past its main industry was farming. The North has always been the home of the manufacturing industry and big business. Now that manufacturing is less important to the US economy, more businesses are re-locating to the South. Many Southern cities are led by black mayors. Although black Americans are more prominent in politics, no black American has ever been elected president.

Martin Luther King
Pre-reading activity

What do you know?

1 What do you know about Martin Luther King? Tick the correct statements:
  a He was a black American leader. ☐
  b He was a black American sportsman. ☐
  c He was a member of the US government. ☐
  d He fought for equal rights for black Americans. ☐
  e In a famous speech he said 'I have a dream'. ☐
  f He was killed. ☐
  g He believed that violence was necessary to change bad laws. ☐

2 Can you match the people with the descriptions?

1 Jesse Jackson	a black musician and composer
2 Malcolm X	b world champion boxer
3 Duke Ellington	c first black woman to be US Secretary of State for Foreign Affairs
4 Muhammad Ali	d black leader who believed that using violence was the only way to get equal rights
5 Condoleezza Rice	e friend and supporter of Martin Luther King

3 What do you think? Give your answers to these questions.
  a **Slavery**
     Why do people want to own slaves?
  b **Equality**
     Why did it take so long for black Americans to have the same rights as white Americans?
  c **Fighting**
     When he was fighting to get equal rights for black people, Martin Luther King went to prison many times. What does this tell you about him?
  d **Rights**
     Which of these rights are the most important?
     The right to vote
     The right to education
     The right to say what you want
     The right to do what you want

To the teacher

Aim: To prepare students to read about Martin Luther King's life and times
Time: 15–20 minutes
Organization: Use a picture of Martin Luther King. Ask students if they know who it is. Then ask them to do Exercise 1 either individually or in pairs.
Key 1: Students should tick Statements a, d, e, and f. Explain that although the book is mainly about Martin Luther King's struggle to gain civil rights for blacks in America, the book tells the story of many other people

who were important in the civil rights movement. Ask them to do Exercise 2. Don't spend too much time on this and tell students not to worry if they don't know many of these people. They will learn about them in the book.
Key 2: 1e; 2d; 3a; 4b; 5c.
Exercise 3 is meant to provoke discussion and get students thinking about some of the ideas that the life of Martin Luther King brings up. Encourage students to express their opinions on these ideas.

Martin Luther King
While reading activity

Spot the mistakes

Read this summary of Chapter 3, Slavery and the South, and correct the mistakes.

Between 1700 and 1850 millions of African men and women were taken from their homes. In America they were sold to white farmers in the South and worked in factories. The white farmers gave the slaves food, clothes, and houses and paid them well. But many slaves ran away from their owners and went back to Africa.

Slaves sometimes fought against their owners. In Liberia, Toussaint L'Ouverture, a black slave, fought a battle against the French.

By 1860 there were more than a million slaves in the South. But more and more people thought that slavery was wrong. The Declaration of Independence said that all people were free to own slaves. Many Northern states ended slavery. In the South slave-owners wanted to keep their slaves but they were not ready to go to war for the right to keep slaves.

Now write a summary of the first part of Chapter 4. Include five mistakes. When you have written it, give it to someone to correct.

_____

_____

_____

_____

_____

To the teacher

Where: At the end of chapter 4

Aim: To consolidate comprehension of two important elements in the background to the life of Martin Luther King – slavery and the American Civil War

Time: 30 minutes

Organization: Make a copy of this worksheet for each student. Ask students to look at the summary and say what it's about. Correct the first mistake with the class. Then ask them to rewrite the summary correcting the remaining mistakes. Allow 10 minutes for this. When students have corrected the mistakes elicit the correct summary from the class. Now ask students to write a summary of the first part of Chapter 4, that is, up to :

By the beginning of the twentieth century a quarter of blacks lived outside the South, mostly in big Northern cities. Remind them that they should include five mistakes, so that it looks like the summary of Chapter 3. When students have written their summaries, ask them to

swap them with their neighbours. Students correct the 'mistakes', as in the first part of the activity.

Key: The corrected summary should look like this: Between 1500 and 1850 millions of African men and women were taken from their homes. In America they were sold to white farmers in the South and worked on *cotton and sugar* farms. The white farmers gave the slaves food, clothes, and houses. But many slaves ran away from their owners and *were caught*.

Slaves sometimes fought against their owners. In *Haiti*, Toussaint L'Ouverture, a black slave, fought a battle against the French.

By 1860 there were *four* million slaves in the South. But more and more people thought that slavery was wrong. The Declaration of Independence said that all people were free *and equal*. Many Northern states ended slavery. In the South slave-owners wanted to keep their slaves *and they were ready* to go to war for the right to keep slaves.

Martin Luther King

After reading activity

Complete the descriptions

1 *Match the phrases to the people.*

President Truman	ordered troops to stop black children from going to school
W.E.B. Dubois	used dogs against black protesters
Orval Faubus	ended segregation in the US army
Bull Connor	became President of the USA after Kennedy
Lyndon B. Johnson	wanted black Americans to return to Africa

2 *Complete these sentences with either the name of a person or a description of what he/ she did.*

Bobby Seale	
	was President of the USA during the Civil War
James Baldwin	
	wrote a song for Martin Luther King's birthday
James Earl Ray	

To the teacher

Aim: To remind students of the role of various figures in the story of Black emancipation

Time: 20 minutes

Organization: Ask students to work in pairs to match the people and the descriptions. Then ask students to say which of these people were in favour of what Martin Luther King was working for and which were against. Encourage discussion here.

Key 1:

Orval Faubus, ordered troops to stop black children from going to school

Bull Connor, used dogs against black protesters

President Truman, ended segregation in the US army

Lyndon B. Johnson, became President of the USA after Kennedy was killed

W.E.B. Dubois, wanted black Americans to return to Africa

There is more scope here for variation, but the table might look something like this:

Key 2:

Bobby Seale, was a leader of the Black Panthers

Abraham Lincoln, was President of the USA during the Civil War

James Baldwin, wrote The fire next time./Was a Black writer

Stevie Wonder, wrote a song for Martin Luther King's birthday

James Earl Ray, was sent to prison for killing Martin Luther King

Moondial

Helen Cresswell

Introduction

Moondial
HELEN CRESSWELL
OXFORD BOOKWORMS
3

> **This ungraded summary is for the teacher's use only and should not be given to students.**

The story

Minty (Araminta) is staying with her Aunt Mary in the country. Her mother has had a serious car accident and lies in a coma in hospital. One day Minty goes to visit Belton House, a large house near her aunt's house. Once the home of a rich family, the house – and gardens – are now open to the public. She meets the gatekeeper, World, who mysteriously asks her if she is the one who is going to let the children free. 'What children?' she wonders.

In the garden there is a sundial. Without knowing why, Minty, standing next to the statue, murmurs the word 'Moondial'. This seems to send her back in time more than a hundred years.

The first person she meets is a boy, Tom. Each thinks that the other is a ghost, although when they touch they both seem real enough. Tom works as a servant in the house, and is clearly not well treated. He has a younger sister, Dorrie, who he is very concerned about.

That evening Minty returns to the gardens again, and again uses the Moondial to go back in time. She meets a young girl, Sarah, who is clearly frightened of her, and who is quickly called into the house by somebody. She then meets Tom again, and she realises that while Tom is from an earlier time, Sarah is probably from another hundred years before him. After more time-travelling, Minty discovers that Sarah has a birthmark on her face and is being persecuted because of this. The people in her time, both children and adults, think that she is a devil's child, and will have nothing to do with her.

Minty's mother remains in a coma, but Minty starts to make a cassette recording of her story for her to listen to when she starts to recover.

A strange and sinister woman, Miss Raven, comes to stay with Aunt Mary. Miss Raven is very interested in ghosts, and on one visit to the Sarah's time in the past, Minty discovers that she, too, must be a time-traveller – for she is also the woman who looks after – and terrorises – Sarah.

Tom and Minty realise that they have to free Sarah in some way. Minty also feels that she has to free Tom and Dorrie, both of whom are clearly ill. Indeed she realises that both Tom and Dorrie are going to die soon – she has already discovered Tom's small gravestone in the graveyard. Tom and Minty meet by the Moondial for one last time, and manage to make contact with Sarah. They are able to show her that she is not a devil's child. Tom's sister Dorrie appears, and Tom, Dorrie and Sarah disappear again out of Minty's view. In some way she has freed the three ghosts.

When she returns to her Aunt Mary's house, she discovers that the evil Miss Raven has gone, and that her mother is out of her coma and wants to see her.

Background to the story

The story spans three times in history and the children who live in them. Minty is a modern girl with the advantages – and problems – of her time. Tom and Dorrie are living in Victorian times – Tom clearly died in 1871. Being from a poor family they are destined to work as servants and almost certainly to an early death from disease. Sarah is clearly from a rich family and from a time perhaps a hundred years before Tom and Dorrie. She lives in an age where superstition and witchcraft are widespread, and where a blemish like a birthmark becomes a cause for terror and persecution. The setting of the story in the real location of Belton House (which is used as the background in the illustrations) adds realism.

Moondial
Pre-reading activity

Who's who?

1 Match the words with the pictures.

a Mr World was sitting near the entrance.

b The woman saw Sarah's purple face and screamed.

c There stood a small girl, wearing a cloak.

d 'That's – me?'

e Suddenly Minty felt cold air pass over her.

f 'I must go!' Tom said. 'Coming?'

g Warm hand met warm hand.

2 Now write in the names of the people.

a .... is a boy who lives more than one hundred years ago. He is not a rich boy, and he lives in a big house where he is a servant.

b .... is a girl who lives in modern times–- but she meets children who live hundreds of years ago.

c .... is an old man who lives in modern times, but knows a lot about the past.

d .... lives more than two hundred years ago. She is quite young and wears a long cloak and often has her head covered.

To the teacher

Aim: To familiarize the students with the setting and characters

Time: 10–15 minutes

Organization: Give one copy of the worksheet to each student or group of students. Ask them to match the words with the pictures. From the results of this matching activity they should be able to write in the names of the characters in Activity 2.

Key: Activity 1: 1e, 2g, 3a, 4c, 5f, 6b, 7d.

Activity 2: a Tom, b Minty, c Mr World, d Sarah.

Moondial

While reading activity

What will happen next?

Miss Raven

Chases Minty and makes her a prisoner.

Disappears.

Remains in the past with Sarah.

Becomes a good person and a friend of Aunt Mary.

Your own idea.

Minty

Will never return to Belton House.

Will save Sarah from Miss Vole.

Will bring Tom and Sarah into modern times.

Will stay in the past with Tom.

Will stay in the past with Sarah.

Your own idea.

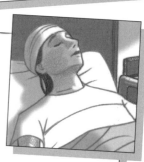

Kate

Gets better and comes to Belton.

Helps Minty to help Tom and Sarah.

Dies.

Stays in hospital for a long time.

Your own idea.

Sarah

Comes to live with Minty in modern times.

Is too frightened to meet Minty again.

Dies.

Kills Miss Vole and escapes from Belton House.

Your own idea.

Tom

Is too frightened to meet Minty again.

Brings Dorrie to Belton House to live with him.

Dies.

Becomes a footman.

Your own idea.

To the teacher

Where: At the end of Chapter 5
Aim: To encourage predictions on the development of the story and its characters
Time: 15–20 minutes

Organization: Give one copy of the worksheet to each student or group of students. Ask the students to make their predictions on what will happen to each of the characters. They may want to retain their predictions to compare with what actually happens in the story.

Moondial
After reading activity

Order the events

	EVENT	ORDER
a	Minty and Miss Raven visit the garden.	
b	Tom comes to visit Minty in her time.	
c	Minty meets World.	
d	Minty starts putting the story onto cassette for her mother.	
e	World tells Minty that the Moondial shows a battle between Time and Love.	
f	Minty visits her mother for the first time in hospital.	
g	Minty and her mother come to Belton.	*1*
h	Minty holds up the mirror to Miss Vole's face.	
i	Minty sees the faceless children chasing Sarah for the first time.	
j	Minty sees Sarah for the first time.	
k	Minty's mother wakes up.	
l	Minty and Tom follow Sarah into Belton House.	
m	Minty and her mother visit Belton churchyard.	
n	Miss Raven leaves.	
o	Minty sees the Moondial and meets Tom.	
p	Minty and Tom show Sarah that she is beautiful.	
q	Minty sees that Miss Vole and Miss Raven are the same person.	
r	Miss Raven comes to stay.	
s	Minty's mother has a car crash.	
t	Minty visits the kitchens with Tom.	

To the teacher

Aim: To order, revise, remember what has been read, summarize

Time: 10–20 minutes

Organization: Give one copy of the worksheet to each student or group of students. Ask them to try and remember the order in which events happened, without looking at the book. Once they have agreed an order, they may wish to go back and check that they have remembered correctly by referring to the book.

Key: 1g, 2m, 3s, 4c, 5o, 6f, 7j, 8t, 9b, 10d, 11i, 12r, 13a, 14l, 15q, 16e, 17p, 18h, 19n, 20k.

On the Edge

Gillian Cross

Introduction

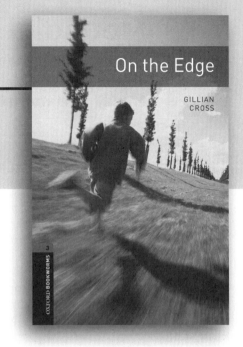

On the Edge

GILLIAN CROSS

The story

One day thirteen-year old Liam Shakespeare, also known as Tug, is kidnapped and drugged on his way home from a long run. His mother Harriet is a famous TV journalist.

When Tug wakes up he discovers that his hair has been cut, and dyed black, to disguise his identity. A man called Doyle and a woman who calls herself 'Ma' are his kidnappers. They have taken him to a cottage in the countryside where they try to convince him that he is their son, 'Phillip', and that he has bumped his head and lost his memory.

Meanwhile, Jinny, a girl from the village nearby is suspicious of the noise that she heard the night of Tug's arrival when she and her father were trapping rabbits in a field close by to the kidnapper's house. She becomes more suspicious when she hears 'Ma' lie about that night to people in the village.

Because of this, she goes to investigate and although she is warned off by Doyle she manages to hear 'Phillip' shouting for help from his bedroom window in the cottage.

'Ma' punishes 'Phillip' for trying to shout for help and hits him hard across the face. Doyle is very angry and guards him closely, threatening him with a gun.

Jinny is determined to find out the truth about the people in the cottage but her friend Keith thinks that she does not have enough facts. However, he finally asks his father, a policeman, for help when Jinny finds a paper aeroplane with the words 'Help!' written on it.

Keith, his father and Jinny go to the cottage but 'Ma' and Doyle convince Keith's father that everything is OK and that 'Phillip' is not very intelligent. Jinny knows something is very wrong because 'Phillip' manages to mouth the word 'Help!' to her; she also realises that the newspaper photograph of the missing boy Liam Shakespeare looks very like 'Phillip' – only the hair is different.

As Jinny watches and listens to the news, it appears that Doyle and 'Ma' belong to an illegal group called 'Free People' who wish to destroy family life. The group eventually offer to free Liam only if all children under the age of sixteen are put into special children's homes – away from their families.

Jinny finally convinces Liam's mother, Harriet, that her son is being held in the cottage. Harriet in turn explains that the motive for the kidnapping to Jinny: Harriet has discovered that 'Free People' are going to blow up the most important family in Britain, the Royal Family and if she tells the police what she knows, the group will kill Liam.

Finally, Jinny and her father, Keith and his father try to rescue Liam from the cottage but as they are about to succeed Doyle suddenly returns to the cottage and takes Jinny prisoner too.

The plot to kill the Royal Family has failed because Harriet has told the police and Doyle now wants to kill Liam. He and 'Ma' take Liam and Jinny to a local cliff known as the Edge where 'Ma' intends to shoot Liam as he goes on the last run of his life. Jinny suddenly distracts 'Ma' and at that moment she is shot by the police as she aims her rifle. She misses Liam. When Doyle tries to pick up the rifle, 'Ma' throws it over the cliff because she has changed her mind about killing Liam. He survives unhurt and runs along the Edge, free at last.

Background to the story

Kidnapping by armed groups is a very common occurrence in today's world although it does not happen very often in Britain. Demands are usually politically linked and often related to the release of other members of the group held in prison. In some countries, the motive is more financial and large ransoms are paid for the release of kidnap victims.

On the Edge
Pre-reading activity

Match the words with the pictures

a 'I was looking for – for – mushrooms,' Jinny said.

b 'There's no dog here,' smiled the man

c 'You're my only hope!' said Harriet.

d Doyle sat by the door, cleaning his gun.

e Slowly Tug turned to look at himself.

f The cottage was almost hidden by trees.

g The television was just starting.

h There was a high window, with strong bars across it.

To the teacher

Aim: To familiarize students with the setting and characters

Time: 15 minutes

Organization: Give one copy of the worksheet to each student or to each pair of students. Ask the students to match the picture with the correct caption. When they have matched the pictures and the captions, ask them:

1 How many different people appear altogether in the pictures?

2 Who are they or what are their relationships? Then ask students to look again at the pictures and put them in order as they think they occur in the story (tell them that picture number 1 is also the first in the sequence). Ask them also to predict the story in general terms.

Key: 1g, 2h, 3b, 4e, 5a, 6d, 7c, 8f

On the Edge
While reading activity

Order the events

	EVENT	ORDER
a	Jinny goes to the cottage to investigate.	
b	Tug goes for a run.	*1*
c	Tug looks at himself in the mirror.	
d	Jinny hears hammering from the cottage.	
e	Ma hits Tug on the face.	
f	Tug calls the Hare-woman 'Ma'.	
g	Tug wakes up in the cottage.	
h	Tug throws a dart out of the window.	
i	Jinny sees the Hare-woman.	
j	Doyle tells Jinny not to come near the cottage again.	
k	Jinny tells Keith about the strange things happening at the cottage.	

To the teacher

Aim: To revise the plot so far
Where: At the end of page 23
Time: 10 minutes
Organization: Hand out the worksheet to students and ask them in groups or pairs to arrange the events in the correct order. Each pair or group must reach a consensus and if there is time, put pairs or groups together and ask them to reach a new consensus.
Key: 1b, 2d, 3g, 4c, 6f, 7a, 8j, 9e, 10k, 11h

On the Edge

After reading activity

Who said what, to whom, where and what about?

	WHO?	WHO TO?	WHERE?	WHAT ABOUT?
1 'From the village you can't hear anything that happens up here.'				
2 'You hit your head and you've forgotten a few things.'				
3 'You usually call me *Ma*. And your breakfast will be cold soon.'				
4 'You see, I was looking for mushrooms.'				
5 'Now you learn to obey orders.'				
6 'We'll take the police car, drive to the cottage and just ask a few questions.'				
7 'You're my only hope!'				
8 'We just wanted to invite you to our harvest party this evening.'				
9 'Suppose that this day is the last day of your life.'				
10 'Run, Tug, run! You're free!'				

To the teacher

Aim: To focus students' attention back on the characters

Time: 15–20 minutes

Organization: Give each student or group of students a copy of the chart. ask them to identify who said these words, who to, where and about what.

Key: 1: Joe to Jinny, in the field next to the cottage, about noises coming from cottage.; 2: Doyle to Tug in Tug's room, trying to explain what has happened to Tug.; 3: Ma to Tug in Tug's room, trying to convince Tug that he is someone else called Phillip.; 4: Jinny to Doyle in the field by the cottage, Jinny was investigating ....; 5: Ma to Tug in his room, Ma is hitting Tug for shouting out of the window.; 6: Keith's dad to Jinny and Keith at Keith's house about the plan to rescue Tug; 7: Harriet to Jinny about saving Tug; 8: Jinny to Tug at the kidnappers cottage trying to rescue Tug; 9: Doyle to Tug on the Edge as he tells to start running; 10: Ma to Tug on the Edge as she saves his life.

A Pair of Ghostly Hands and Other Stories

Retold by Diane Mowat

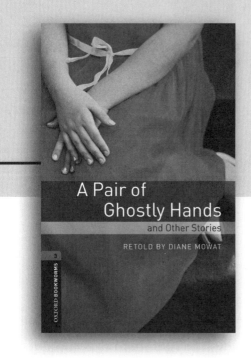

A Pair of Ghostly Hands
and Other Stories

RETOLD BY DIANE MOWAT

Introduction

> **This ungraded summary is for the teacher's use only and should not be given to students.**

The stories

A Pair of Ghostly Hands. Aunt Emily rents a house in Cornwall from a farmer, Mr Hosking. The housekeeper, Mrs Carkeek, who has lived in the house for many years, seems a kind, sensible woman. The house is kept very clean, and Aunt Emily does not understand when the cleaning takes place – no matter how early she gets up in the morning, the house has always been cleaned since the previous evening. One day she finds a small washbasin in a room at the back of the house – she wants to get some water there for some flowers, but the tap doesn't work. She discovers that Mrs Carkeek has blocked the pipe to the tap and despite Mrs Carkeek's objections she removes the blockage. In the middle of the night, Emily is woken up by the sound of running water. She sees two hands, washing themselves under the tap. The next morning, Mrs Carkeek explains that the hands belong to Margaret, a seven-year-old girl who died more than twenty years ago. She is the person who cleans the house every night. Aunt Emily stays in the house keeping the secret of Margaret's helpful hands.

Lost Hearts. Stephen, an eleven-year-old orphan, goes to live with his cousin, Mr Abney. The housekeeper tells Stephen that his cousin is a kind man, who has taken in two other young children, a boy and a girl, both of whom stayed in the house for some time, and then disappeared. Stephen has strange dreams, in which he sees the ghosts of a boy and a girl. One day, Mr Abney asks Stephen to come and meet him, late at night in the library. When Stephen arrives, Mr Abney is dead. Stephen discovers, from papers left on his desk, that Mr Abney believed that he could get magical powers by eating the hearts of three children. Stephen was to be the last of the three – but was saved by the ghosts of the two other children.

Mrs Amworth. Mrs Amworth comes to live in a quiet English village on the death of her husband in India. Some time after her arrival, a boy falls ill, and the narrator and Mr Urcombe, who both live in the village, believe that a vampire has been drinking his blood. One night, the narrator wakes up and sees Mrs Amworth's face floating outside his window. The two men meet Mrs Amworth in the street and confront her with their suspicions. When Urcombe makes the sign of the cross she steps back in horror into the path of a car, and is killed. But the vampire continues to attack. One night the two men follow Mrs Amworth to the graveyard, dig up the body and kill her for a second, final, time.

The Waxwork. Raymond Hewson, a newspaper reporter, arranges to spend the night in the Murderer's Room at the Waxworks, so that he can write an article about it for a newspaper. One of the most frightening waxworks in the room is that of Dr Bourdette, who killed people with a razor, and who has never been caught. During the night, Hewson imagines that the waxwork speaks to him, telling him that he is not a waxwork but is in fact Dr Bourdette who is hiding from the police. He approaches Hewson, who is too terrified to move, takes out a razor, and cuts his throat. The next morning, Hewson is found dead in the Murderer's Room – but there is not a mark on him.

John Charrington's Wedding. John Charrington and May Forster are going to be married, but Charrington has to go away to visit a sick uncle just before the wedding. He promises May that he will be back in time for the wedding – dead or alive. He does arrive in time for the wedding, looking deathly pale, and when the carriage arrives back at the Forster's home, only May is inside, her eyes filled with fear, and her hair white as snow. We learn that Charrington was killed in an accident on the way to the wedding, and May married his ghost.

A Pair of Ghostly Hands andOther Stories

Pre-reading activity

Match the stories with the events

These are the titles of the stories in this book.

A PAIR OF GHOSTLY HANDS

THE WAXWORK

LOST HEARTS

MRS AMWORTH

JOHN CHARRINGTON'S WEDDING

Look at the events and write the titles of the stories.

EVENT		TITLE
1	A newspaper reporter spends the night in a very strange room.	
2	A woman sees two hands washing themselves under a tap.	
3	A woman dies a week after she gets married.	
4	Two children disappear from a rich man's house.	
5	A house is cleaned every night.	
6	A woman who is a vampire lives in an English village.	
7	A man promises to get married – dead or alive.	
8	A man is killed by the ghosts of two children.	
9	A murderer kills again – or perhaps he doesn't.	
10	Two men kill a vampire.	
11	A man needs children's hearts for magic.	
12	A woman lives happily for three years in a house with a ghost.	
13	The death bell rings in a church.	
14	A ghost is helpful, and not frightening.	

To the teacher

Aim: To pre-teach some of the vocabulary and to help students begin to understand the contexts of the stories

Time: 10–15 minutes

Organization: Give one copy of the worksheet to each student or each group of students. Check through the sentences and check any unknown meanings with the class. Alternatively, the students could look up any difficult words in their dictionaries. Ask the students to write the titles of the stories in the spaces next to the events. When everyone has finished, discuss the answers with the class. Give no indication as to whether the students have guessed correctly or not.

Key: 1 The Waxwork, 2 A Pair of Ghostly Hands, 3 John Charrington's Wedding, 4 Lost Hearts, 5 A Pair of Ghostly Hands, 6 Mrs Amworth, 7 John Charrington's Wedding, 8 Lost Hearts, 9 The Waxwork, 10 Mrs Amworth, 11 Lost Hearts, 12 A Pair of Ghostly Hands, 13 John Charrington's Wedding, 14 A Pair of Ghostly Hands.

A Pair of Ghostly Hands and Other Stories

While reading activity

What next?

A PAIR OF GHOSTLY HANDS			YES	NO
	1	There is a ghost in the house.		
What happens after page 5?	2	Mrs Carkeek is a ghost.		
	3	The ghost cleans the house.		
	4	The ghost frightens Aunt Emily away from the house.		
Tick the boxes.	5	Aunt Emily frightens the ghost away from the house.		
	6			

LOST HEARTS			YES	NO
	1	There are ghosts in the cellar.		
What happens after page 17?	2	The ghosts kill Stephen.		
	3	The ghosts kill Mr Abney.		
	4	Stephen runs away from Aswarby Hall.		
Tick the boxes.	5	Something burns down Aswarby Hall.		
	6			

MRS AMWORTH			YES	NO
	1	We discover that Urcombe is a vampire.		
What happens after page 25?	2	We discover that Mrs Amworth is a vampire.		
	3	We discover that Mr Amworth was a vampire.		
	4	People in Maxley start to die.		
Tick the boxes.	5	Urcombe dies.		
	6	Mrs Amworth dies.		
	7			

THE WAXWORK			YES	NO
	1	Mr Hewson sees a ghost.		
What happens after page 40?	2	Mr Hewson dies.		
	3	Mr Hewson sleeps all night and sees nothing.		
	4	Mr Hewson attacks a waxwork.		
Tick the boxes.	5	A waxwork attacks Mr Hewson.		
	6			

To the teacher

Where: At the point on the page where * * * on the page indicate a break in the story

Aim: To give the students the chance to predict where the story is going

Time: 5–10 minutes (for each story)

Organization: Give each student, or group of students a copy of the worksheet for the story that they are reading. Tell them that they must decide what is going to happen in the story. They can write in their own predictions in the blank spaces at the end of the table.

A Pair of Ghostly Hands and Other Stories

After reading activity

Character crosswords

Make character crosswords for these characters.

```
        L O V E D   A U N T   E M I L Y
                        C L E A N E D   T H E   H O U S E
                    N O T   F R I G H T E N I N G
    A   S E V E N - Y E A R - O L D   G I R L
                            W A S H E S   H E R   H A N D S
                S A W   T E R R I B L E   T H I N G S
                D I E D   T W E N T Y   Y E A R S   A G O
            T U R N S   T H E   T A P   O N
```

(circled vertical word: M A R G A R E T)

```
.......... M ....................        .................. D ......................
.......... R ....................        .................. R ......................

............... A ................        .................. B ......................
............... B ................        .................. O ......................
............... N ................        .................. U ......................
............... E ................        .................. R ......................
............... Y ................        .................. D ......................
                                          .................. E ......................
                                          .................. T ......................
                                          .................. T ......................
                                          .................. E ......................

.......... M ....................
.......... R ....................
.......... S ....................        .................. J ......................
                                         .................. O ......................
............... A ................        .................. H ......................
............... M ................        .................. N ......................
............... W ................
............... O ................        .................. C ......................
............... R ................        .................. H ......................
............... T ................        .................. A ......................
............... H ................        .................. R ......................
                                         .................. R ......................
                                         .................. I ......................
                                         .................. N ......................
                                         .................. G ......................
                                         .................. T ......................
                                         .................. O ......................
                                         .................. N ......................
```

The Picture of Dorian Gray

Oscar Wilde

Introduction

> This ungraded summary is for the teacher's use only and should not be given to students.

The story

Basil Hallward, an artist, has painted an excellent portrait of a beautiful young man, Dorian Gray. Lord Henry Wotton thinks it should be exhibited, but Basil says he has put too much of himself into it; he feels strangely drawn to Dorian. Lord Henry is intrigued, and takes Dorian under his wing, telling him how important youth and beauty are. Dorian wishes he could stay young and good-looking for ever, while his portrait grows old. This is, in fact, what happens during his life. He falls in love with a young actress, Sybil, but cruelly rejects her, causing her suicide. He then becomes part of Lord Henry's sophisticated, cold-hearted circle, and loses all his innocence. Everything seems to be going Dorian's way; he is a wealthy gentleman with many friends, and he still looks as young and handsome as ever. Only *he* knows about the portrait he keeps locked up in his attic – the portrait with its dreadful, evil, lined face. One day Basil meets Dorian and asks about rumours he has heard of Dorian's immoral life. Dorian tells him the secret of the portrait, shows it to him, then stabs him to death. In order to get rid of Basil's body, he blackmails a former friend who is a scientist, and who reluctantly agrees to help destroy the body. Sybil's brother James appears, wanting to punish Dorian for Sybil's death, but James is accidentally shot. Now Dorian has nothing to fear, but he has nothing to live for, either. He realizes that he has a beautiful face, but no heart, and in despair he stabs the portrait, trying to free himself from any connection with it. The servants find him dead on the floor, with an old, ugly face, while the portrait of the young and beautiful Dorian hangs untouched on the wall.

Background to the story

The author, Oscar Wilde, was born in 1854 in Dublin, Ireland. He studied at Trinity College, Dublin, and Magdalen College, Oxford. When he graduated, he moved straight into London literary society. There he impressed people with his witty, intelligent conversation, and shocked them with his ideas on art, fashion and taste. He wrote poems, stories, essays and plays. *The Picture of Dorian Gray* is his best-known story, and *The Importance of Being Earnest* is his most famous play. He was imprisoned because of his homosexual behaviour in 1895, and died in 1900.

The story is set almost a hundred years ago, towards the end of the last century, when ladies and gentlemen of good name and wealth had very little to do except give dinner parties, drive around in their carriages, and make clever, amusing conversation. It was a time when it was fashionable to think, or pretend to think, only of beauty, pleasure and selfish enjoyment. For many of the upper classes, poor people, whether servants or actors or street-sweepers, only existed to make life more comfortable or attractive for their masters. It was generally accepted that a gentleman could not cross the class barrier and marry a servant girl or actress, without losing some of his position. The police and other authorities also had great respect for the upper classes, which meant that it was easier for a gentleman to commit serious crimes and escape punishment than it would be today.

The Picture of Dorian Gray
Pre-reading activity

Match the words with the pictures / Storyline

Match the words with the pictures on the next page.

a A man's dead body was pulled from the trees.

b 'Tell me how you have kept your youth and your wonderful beauty, Dorian,' said Lord Henry.

c 'It's the best portrait that you've ever painted,' said Lord Henry.

d Lying on the floor was a dead man, with a knife in his heart.

e 'Oh James, don't be angry with me today,' cried Sybil Vane.

f Dorian stood and listened. He could hear nothing – only the drip, drip of blood onto the floor.

g 'I wish that I could always stay young and that the picture could grow old,' cried Dorian.

h 'I've been looking for you for years – Prince Charming!' said James Vane.

Put these chapter headings in the order in which you think they occur.

The Picture

The Young Man in Love

The Friend

The Sailor

The Hand of a Killer

The Death of Love

The Artist

The Thief of Time

....
....
....
....
....
....
....
....

To the teacher

Aim: To familiarize students with the setting (Match the words with the pictures)/To predict the storyline (Storyline)

Time: 15 minutes (Match the words with the pictures)/15 minutes (Storyline)

Organization: Give one copy of the worksheet to each student or each pair or group of students. Ask the students to match the picture with the correct caption. Now ask students to discuss:

1 Who are some of the people in the story?

2 What do you know or can you imagine about their characters?

After the first pre-reading activity, ask students to put the chapter headings from the book they are going to read in a suitable order for telling a story. Groups should exchange their story ideas. (Do not say whether they are right or wrong.) Later they can look back at this activity and compare their story ideas with what they read.

Key: 1c, 2g, 3e, 4b, 5f, 6h, 7a, 8d.

1

4

7

2

5

8

3

6

The Picture of Dorian Gray

While reading activity

Get it right

Correct the mistakes.

A

Basil Hallward is very pleased with the portrait he has painted of his friend Dorian Gray. Basil would like to be as beautiful as Dorian, and he is going to exhibit the portrait so that everyone in London can see it. Lord Henry meets Dorian, and takes pleasure in helping the young man become a better person. Dorian falls in love with a well-known actress, and they plan to run away together. But before they can marry, she dies, and Dorian remains single and unhappy for the rest of his life.

B

Dorian Gray knows what a beautiful face he has, and he wants to look young and handsome for ever. He learns a lot from Lord Henry, and begins to discover what life is all about. However, he loses interest in Sybil, the young actress, as quickly as he fell in love with her, and he kills her in a moment of anger. His old friend Basil is shocked to discover how cruel and heartless Dorian has become. The picture of the evil, ageing Dorian is kept locked away at the top of Dorian's house, but one day Basil breaks down the door and manages to look at it. When the artist sees how the portrait he painted has changed, he has a heart attack and falls down dead.

C

Lord Henry thinks that life should never be serious, and that it is more fun to be bad than good. He is one of Dorian's best friends, and encourages him to enjoy every wild pleasure that life can offer. Lord Henry knows why Sybil killed herself, and he knows all about the changing portrait in Dorian's upstairs room. He sends Basil to certain death at Dorian's hands, by persuading the artist to ask Dorian about his evil life, and he suggests to Dorian that Alan Campbell could help to get rid of Basil's body. He is far cleverer, and more evil, than Dorian Gray.

Now write your summary here.

....

....

....

....

....

....

....

....

....

....

....

To the teacher

Where: At the end of Chapter 13

Aim: To help with summarizing and revision of reading

Time: 20 minutes

Organization: Give a copy of the three summaries to each student and ask them to find which parts of the summaries are incorrect and which are correct, then to use information taken from the summaries to write their own version. Each summary contains some incorrect information.

The Picture of Dorian Gray

After reading activity

Who's who?

1 Henry Wotton *12 21 25*	**8** A very beautiful and noble lady	**15** Sybil's brother	**22** Paints a portrait of Dorian
2 Basil Hallward	**9** A pretty young actress	**16** A friend of Dorian's when young	**23** Stays good-looking all his life
3 Dorian Gray	**10** A clever scientist	**17** Dorian's mother	**24** Runs away from home to marry a soldier
4 Margaret Devereux	**11** A very good artist	**18** The main character	**25** Encourages Dorian to become evil
5 Sybil Vane	**12** A rich and amusing lord	**19** Dorian's first love	**26** Kills herself
6 James Vane	**13** A gentleman with a young and beautiful face	**20** Once a good friend of Dorian's	**27** Wants to take revenge on Dorian with a guilty secret
7 Alan Campbell	**14** A dark young sailor	**21** A friend of Basil's and Dorian's	**28** Helps to get rid of Basil's body

To the teacher

Aim: To focus attention back on the characters
Time: 20 minutes
Organization: Give each student or group of students a copy of the worksheet. Ask them to match up the names and the information. See how much they can do without referring back to the book.
Key: 1: 12, 21, 25; 2: 11, 16, 22; 3: 13, 18, 23; 4: 8, 17, 24; 5: 9, 19, 26; 6: 14, 15, 27; 7: 10, 20, 28.

The Prisoner of Zenda

Anthony Hope

Introduction

The story

Rudolf Rassendyll is a rich nineteenth-century English aristocrat who is young and idle. He has inherited the blue eyes, long straight nose and dark red hair of the Elphbergs, the royal family of Ruritania, who are distant relatives.

So many people comment on the similarities between the two families that Rudolf finally decides to see his relatives for himself. He goes to Ruritania to attend the coronation of the King. This will be his last adventure before settling down and doing something useful with his life.

His adventure begins when he catches the train from Paris – he sees the beautiful Madame Antoinette de Mauban and learns that she is in love with the Duke of Strelsau, the half brother of the future King.

While on a visit to the grounds around the Duke's castle, Rudolf meets the future King's aides, Captain Sapt and Fritz von Tarlenheim. They are amazed by the physical likeness between Rudolf and the future King and take him to meet him and celebrate the occasion with a party.

The next day, the king cannot be woken from his sleep – the bottle of wine has been drugged by the Duke so that the future King cannot attend his own coronation! Captain Sapt asks Rudolf to impersonate the King and go in his place to the coronation. In the meantime, they hide the sleeping King and his servant.

The coronation is a success and Rudolf is crowned King. Nobody suspects the impersonation particularly Princess Flavia who is destined to marry the King of Ruritania one day.

When Rudolf and the others return to the inn in Zenda, they discover that the King had been kidnapped and taken to the Castle of Zenda by the Duke's men. His servant is dead. When some of the Duke's men return to take away the body, Rudolf and the King's aides fight and kill three of them.

Rudolf agrees to continue his impersonation of the King to keep Duke Michael from killing the King and claiming the throne.

Antoinette de Mauban unexpectedly helps Rudolf by telling him where the King is being kept prisoner. She loves the Duke and does not want him to become King and marry Princess Flavia. While meeting with Antoinette, Rudolf is attacked by the Duke's men but escapes.

In order to maintain the pretence, the King's aides announce that the King is to marry Princess Flavia. The Princess has never really liked the King, but is now surprised as she falls in love. Rudolf feels the same way but cannot tell her the truth.

The Duke's men now try to prevent the wedding by trying to bribe Rudolf into leaving the country. When that fails, Rupert of Hentzua tries to kill Rudolf but only stabs him in his shoulder.

When Rudolf and the King's aides hear that the King is dangerously ill they plan a rescue. In the fight that follows, Rudolf saves the life of the King but is badly injured himself.

Princess Flavia rushes to his side and learns the truth about his identity. She and Rudolf both realise that they must follow different destinies but accept it with a great deal of sadness.

Background to the story

Sir Anthony Hope Hawkins (1863–1933) whose pen-name was Anthony Hope lead a privileged life, attending public school and studying at Oxford University before becoming a lawyer. *The Prisoner of Zenda*, a romantic adventure story published in 1894, has been translated into many different languages and made into plays and films.

The Prisoner of Zenda

Pre-reading activity

Anticipation through chapter titles

The Rassendylls – and the Ephbergs

For love of the King

The colour of men's hair

Back to Zenda

The King goes to his coronation

News of the prisoner

A night outside the castle

My adventures begin

A dangerous plan

His majesty returns to Strelsau

The prisoner and the castle

An adventure with a tea-table

Goodbye to Ruritania

To the teacher

Aim: To familiarize students with setting and to anticipate plot

Time: 15–20 minutes

Organization: Supply the students with the following list of chapter titles, either as individual copies or on an overhead projector. Check to make sure that there are no problems with vocabulary items in the list. Then divide the students into small groups and ask them to speculate as wildly as they can about the meaning of the chapter titles, their connection with one another, and their connection with the title of the book. It is not important whether their guesses are correct or not; they should simply be encouraged to speculate about possible connections. They may be able to come up with an idea of a plot line, but this is not essential. When students have finished, allow each group to outline its ideas in a short verbal report to the class. Give no indication as to whether they have guessed correctly, but let them listen to all the ideas and discuss them if they wish.

The Prisoner of Zenda

While reading activity

Characters and descriptions

Match the characters with the descriptions.

1 Rose
2 Lord Burlesdon
3 Rudolf Rassendyll
4 Madame Antoinette de Mauban
5 Duke Michael of Streslau
6 Princess Flavia
7 Captain Sapt
8 The King of Ruritania

a has black hair
b likes to drink a lot of wine
c is in love with Duke Michael
d is married to Lord Burlesdon
e is tall, dark, and very fashionable
f is the cousin of the King of Ruritania
g is brother to Lord Burlesdon
h is the King of Ruritania's half brother
i works for the King of Ruritania
j wants to marry Princess Flavia

To the teacher

Where: At the end of Chapter 2
Aim: To revise information about the characters
Time: 10–20 minutes

Organization: Give out the worksheets and put students into groups. Ask them to match the two columns. The first one has been done for them.
Key: 1d, 2a, 3g, 4c and e, 5h and j, 6f, 7i, 8b.

STAGE 3

The Prisoner of Zenda
After reading activity

Who said what, to whom, where and what about?

		WHO?	WHO TO?	WHERE?	WHAT ABOUT?
1	'I wonder when you are going to do anything useful.'				
2	'Well done Black Michael . . . I'm not afraid of your wine.'				
3	'You must go to Strelsau and take his place.'				
4	'Stay back . . . I'll show my people that I'm not afraid of them.'				
5	'These men are coming to kill you.'				
6	'Tonight you must ask the Princess to marry.'				
7	'I love you more than my life.'				
8	'He wants you to leave. He'll take you safely out of the country and give you a thousand pounds.'				
9	'Thanks to a very brave Englishman, the King is still alive.'				
10	'Don't kiss him. He is the man you love – but he is not the King.'				

To the teacher

Aim: To focus student's attention back on the characters and plot
Time: 15–20 minutes
Organization: Give each student or group of students a copy of the worksheet. Ask them to complete the table.
Key: 1 Rose to Rudolf his brother's home about his idleness; 2 The King to Captain Sapt in the inn near Zenda about the Duke's gift of wine; 3 Captain Sapt to Rudolf in the inn near Zenda about the impersonation; 4 Rudolf to Captain Sapt while riding to his coronation about the angry crowd; 5 Madame Antoinette de Mauban to Rudolf at her summer house about the Duke's men; 6 Captain Sapt to Rudolf about the Princess Flavia marrying the King; 7-Rudolf to Princess Flavia at the night of the ball when the marriage is announced; 8 Rupert of Hentzau to Rudolf in the garden at Tarlenheim House about the Duke's bribe for him to leave; 9 Fritz to Rudolf at the castle about Rudolf's bravery in saving the King's life; 10 Sapt to Princess Flavia at the castle when she rushes to see the injured Rudolf.

Rabbit-Proof Fence

Doris Pilkington Garimara

Introduction

Rabbit-Proof Fence

DORIS PILKINGTON GARIMARA

OXFORD BOOKWORMS

The story

Rabbit-Proof Fence is set in Western Australia in the 1930s. It is the true story of three half-caste girls Molly, Gracie, and Daisy who have Aboriginal mothers and white fathers. The girls grow up in the bush with their extended Aboriginal families around the government depot of Jigalong.

In the early 1900s the Australian government introduced a new law which said that children of Aboriginal mothers and white fathers should be taken away from their families and sent to Native Settlement schools. They would be taught to behave like white people and forget their Aboriginal background.

As a consequence of this law, a policeman comes to the girls' families in the bush one day. He has a letter saying that Molly, Daisy, and Gracie must be sent to the Moore River Native Settlement 1,600 kilometres away near Perth. Their mothers protest but the girls are taken away on a long journey by car, train, and ship to their new home.

When the girls arrive they make friends with Martha, who explains all about the harsh life at the Native Settlement. She shows the girls the small punishment building where all children who try to escape are sent. She also explains about Moodoo, who tracks and catches anybody who runs away.

Molly immediately vows to leave the Native Settlement. She escapes with Gracie and Daisy and they start to walk north in search of the rabbit-proof fence, which they know will guide them back to Jigalong. The weather is wet so the rain washes away their footprints and stops Moodoo from finding them.

The girls' knowledge of life in the bush helps them to survive the difficult conditions of their journey. Two Mardu men give them some matches and they catch and cook wild animals on open fires in the bush.

News of the girls' escape is put in all the newspapers and Moodoo the tracker and the police look hard for Molly, Daisy, and Gracie – but the girls walk quickly, cover their tracks and avoid all roads and villages. However, the harsh journey becomes too much for the tired Gracie. Even though the girls find and start to follow the rabbit-proof fence, Gracie decides to go her own way and tries to look for her mother in Wiluna.

Molly and Daisy eventually reach home in Jigalong and they disappear into the desert with their Aboriginal families. The authorities realize that there is no point in trying to find the girls as they would only escape again.

Gracie is caught and sent back to the Moore River Native Settlement where she stays.

Background to the story

Rabbit-Proof Fence was written by Doris Pilkington Garimara who is the daughter of Molly. Doris was separated from her mother at the age of four and she was brought up in a Native Settlement. However, she was reunited with her mother, Molly, at the age of twenty-five and also later met her Aunt Daisy. It was Aunt Daisy who told Doris the details of their long walk to Jigalong and Doris vowed to write down the details of the story.

Rabbit-Proof Fence was published in 1996 and made into a film in 2002. It started a wide debate in Australia about the 'lost generations' of Aborigines. It has been estimated that up to 100,000 Aboriginal children were moved from their families between 1910 and 1970. Most of the children were under the age of five and they were sent to Native Settlements in order to learn to be low grade domestic helpers or farm workers. The government believed that the children would have a better life if they left their families in the bush and learned to live like white Europeans.

STAGE 3

Rabbit-Proof Fence
Pre-reading activity

Prediction – What is the rabbit-proof fence?

1 *Look at the map of Western Australia on the right. Mark in coloured pen the rabbit-proof fence.*

2 *Guess the answers to these questions about the rabbit-proof fence.*

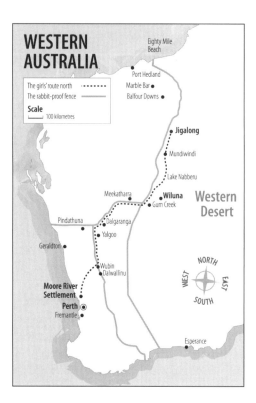

1 How long is the rabbit-proof fence?
   a 834 km   **b** 1,834 km   **c** 2,834 km

2 Where does the rabbit-proof fence run from?
   a From the south to the north coast.
   b From the east to the north coast.
   c From the east to the west coast.

3 When was the rabbit-proof fence built?
   a 1507   **b** 1707   **c** 1907

4 Why was the rabbit-proof fence built?
   a To keep the rabbits in Western Australia.
   b To keep the rabbits out of Western Australia.
   c To stop people stealing rabbits from farms in Western Australia.

5 Who uses the rabbit-proof fence as an important landmark?
   a The Mardu – the Aboriginal people who live in Western Australia.
   b The white farmers who live in the bush.
   c The policemen who fly in planes over the bush.

Now read page 1 of Rabbit-Proof Fence to check your answers.

3 *Read the introduction inside Rabbit-Proof Fence which begins:* **The Aborigines were the first people in Australia . . .**
   a Look back at the map above. Mark in coloured pen the girls' journey home.
   b Why do you think the rabbit-proof fence is so important to the girls on their journey?
   c How do you think the girls feel when they first find the rabbit-proof fence?

To the teacher

Aim: To encourage prediction about the story and its setting
Time: 40 minutes
Organization: Put the students into pairs. Give out one copy of the worksheet to each pair. Ask students to look carefully at the map. Encourage them to speculate what the area of Australia around Jigalong may be like: a vast, hot desert.

   Ask students to mark in colour the rabbit-proof fence (note that it has three branches). Then ask them

to guess the answers to the questions and check their ideas with the text on page 1of the book.

   Finally ask them to read the introduction, then look back at the map / key and mark in colour the girls' journey. They must guess / imagine the answers to b and c as the information is not in the text.
Key: 2 1 b, 2 a, 3 c, 4 b, 5 a, 3 b The rabbit-proof fence can help guide the girls back to their home at Jigalong.
c Very happy and relieved.

Missing

MISSING –
Aboriginal Girls

NAMES..

AGES...

DESCRIPTION..

....

CLOTHES...

The girls ran away from..

....

They are travelling on...

....

They are trying to get home to...

....

They may be near..

....

If you see the girls, ...

....

Mr A. O. Neville

Chief Protector of Aborigines, Perth

August 1931

To the teacher

Where: At the end of Chapter 5
Aim: To consolidate comprehension of the story up to the end of chapter 5
Time: 30 minutes
Organization: Explain to students that they are going to write a 'missing' poster for the girls. Ask the class what information they would need to put on it.

Put the students into groups of three. Hand out one copy of the worksheet per group. Ask students to look back through the story and make rough notes to complete the poster. Students then fill in a 'best' copy. Encourage students to write as much information as possible. For example: They are travelling on foot and they are walking long distances every day. They may be near the rabbit-proof fence because this will guide them home.

Note that the girls' ages can be found on page 5 of the book.

Rabbit-Proof Fence

After reading activity

Spot the mistakes

Read the newspaper article about the girls' journey home. There are some mistakes in the article. Can you find them? The first one has been done for you and there are ten others for you to find and correct.

Aboriginal girls arrive home after incredible journey

Two young Aboriginal girls, Molly and Daisy are reported to have arrived home after ~~cycling~~ *walking* 600 kilometres across Eastern Australia.

The girls were sent to Moore River Native Settlement near Perth but they ran away and decided to return home to Wubin. At the start, there were three girls but one of them, Gracie, became very tired. She left the others and went to look for her father in Wiluna.

As soon as the girls escaped from the Native Settlement, a tracker and some policemen started to search for them. However, they couldn't find the girls' tracks because of the windy weather.

When they started on their long walk, Molly knew that it was important to go south. She was looking for and eventually found the kangaroo-proof fence, which would lead them back to their home.

Molly, Daisy, and Gracie were able to survive their incredible journey because they knew how to live in the bush. They cooked and ate different wild plants and drank river water. At night they built shelters to sleep in.

During the journey, the girls met several people including a woman called Mrs Flanagan. 'They came to my farmhouse one day,' she explained. 'They were very hungry and wet so I gave them food and some warm dresses to put on. I decided not to phone the superintendent about them.'

The girls have now disappeared back into the bush with their Aboriginal families.

Aim: To revise key elements of the story

Time: 40 minutes

Organization: Put the students in pairs and ask them to make brief notes about key events in Rabbit-Proof Fence. During class feedback brainstorm the main points of the story and note them on the board. Give out a copy of the worksheet to each pair. Ask them to identify and correct the ten mistakes in the article. Class feedback.

Key: 600 – 1,600, Eastern – Western, Wubin – Jigalong, father – mother, windy – rainy / wet, plants – animals, south – north, kangaroo – rabbit, warm dresses – warm coats, decided not to phone – decided to phone.

The Railway Children

Edith Nesbit

Introduction

The story

Three children, Roberta (also known as Bobbie), Peter and Phyllis, live happily with their parents in London until one day, on Peter's birthday, their father receives some bad news and has to go away immediately. The children and their mother leave London and go to live in the country.

The children soon settle down. They love the railway station and the railway line which runs nearby and make friends with Perks, the porter. Everyday they wave at the 9.15 train, wishing that it will take their love to their father. Each day an old gentleman waves back at them from the train.

The railway soon becomes the scene of many adventures. One day Peter and his sisters are caught stealing coal by the Station Master – he tells them not to do it again.

Soon after, the children's mother falls ill and the doctor tells her that she needs special food and medicine to get better. As she is poor, the children decide to ask the old gentleman on the train for help. That evening a large box arrives with the things the doctor recommended – including twelve roses.

One day after her birthday, Bobbie decides to take Peter's broken toy steam engine to be repaired. While Bobbie is climbing onto a train to speak to the fireman and driver about the toy, the train starts and the two men do not see her fall back into the coal truck. The driver and fireman are surprised to find Bobbie there but mend Peter's toy engine.

But the railway can be a dangerous place too. One day the side of a hill near the railway slips down across the track. The children are too far from the station to warn anybody so they cut up the girls' red petticoats to make warning flags for the next train – Bobbie bravely stands on the track to stop the train. The directors of the railway company hold a special ceremony soon afterwards to thank the children for saving the lives of the people on the train.

The children are always ready to think of other people and on Perks' birthday they give him a surprise.

They collect presents for him and because Perks is so popular, many people are happy to give something. But Perks is angry because he thinks people believe he is too poor to look after his own family. However, he soon realises that his neighbours wish only to be kind to him.

One day Bobbie discovers her father has been imprisoned for five years as a spy. Her mother explains that one of Father's enemies put secret papers in his desk so that the police would find them. Bobbie writes to ask the old gentleman for help.

The children are involved in another adventure on the railway. A school-boy, called Jim, is taking part in a cross–country race when he hurts his leg in the railway tunnel. The three children rush into the tunnel to help and Bobbie stays with him. Jim is carried back to the children's house and the next day his grandfather comes to visit. He is the old gentleman from the train! He gives Mother the job of nursing Jim until he is better. And before he leaves he tells Bobbie that he has been working to help her father.

One day soon after, when the children are waving at the 9.15 train they notice that everyone is waving back at them. Bobbie realises that something good has happened and goes to the station later in the morning in time to see three people get off the train and find that one of them is her father, free at last!

Background to the story

Edith Nesbit (1858–1924) was an English writer of children's stories, many of which are still popular today. *The Railway Children* (1906) was made into a film in 1970. Another children's story by Edith Nesbit, *Five Children and It* is available in the Oxford Bookworms Series (see the Oxford Graded Readers Catalogue), although at a slightly lower level.

The Railway Children

Pre-reading activity

Match the words with the pictures

a 'I don't like it!' said Phyllis.

b 'Now I've caught you, you young thief!'

c A man with a cart took their boxes.

d And there was the railway, with its shining lines, telegraph wires and posts, and signals.

e Hands and handkerchiefs and newspapers waved from every window in the train.

f Suddenly half the hillside was moving.

g There was also some wine, two chickens, and twelve red roses.

h They spent a happy two hours with the Porter.

To the teacher

Aim: To familiarize students with the story and its setting

Time: 10–15 minutes

Organization: Give one copy of the worksheet to each student or group of students. Ask the students to match the words with the appropriate picture.

When the students have completed this task, check the answers with them. Ask students to make a list of all the characters who appear in these pictures and then decide on a possible order for the pictures.

Key: 1g, 2d, 3e, 4c, 5h, 6b, 7a, 8f.

The Railway Children

While reading activity

True or false? / What happens next?

True or false?

		TRUE	FALSE
1	The railway children lived happily with their parents in London.		
2	Their father suddenly goes away on a long holiday.		
3	The children and their mother go to live in the country.		
4	When they arrive at their new home there is a fire and a hot meal waiting for them.		
5	To make money their mother makes dresses.		
6	The station master takes Peter and his sisters to the police for stealing coal.		

What happens next?

Mother
Mother goes to hospital.
Mother gets better.
Your suggestion . . .

Old Gentleman
He sends them money to help them.
He visits them.
Your suggestion . . .

Bobbie
Bobbie goes to work as a nurse with the doctor.
Bobbie writes stories for magazines.
Your suggestion . . .

The family
Mother is too ill to stay in the country so they return to London.
The children go to stay with their grandparents while their mother goes to hospital.
Your suggestion . . .

To the teacher

Where: At the end of page 14 and at the end of page 18
Aim: To help students understand the plot; to predict events in the following section.
Time: 15–20 minutes
Organization: When the students have read up to page 14, give them the worksheet and ask them to decide whether the statements are true or false. Later when students have read up to page 18 ask them to predict what will happen next before reading to confirm.
Key: 1T, 2F, 3T, 4F, 5F, 6F.

The Railway Children

After reading activity

Who said what, to whom, and what about?

Complete the table.

		WHO?	WHO TO?	WHAT ABOUT?
1	'I'll mend it on Saturday, and you can all help me.'			
2	'We can't take everything . . . Just the necessary things. We have to play "being poor."'			
3	'Now I've caught you, you young thief!'			
4	'I'll write a letter to the old gentleman and thank him.'			
5	'Look some of the trees are moving too.'			
6	'I'm not having anything of it! We've managed all these years, asking people for nothing . . .'			
7	'I thank you, Madam, for welcoming me to your house today.'			
8	'You don't believe it, do you. You don't believe Daddy is a spy?'			
9	'I think I've broken my leg.'			
10	'I saw it in the paper, and I've never been so pleased about anything in all my life.'			

To the teacher

Aim: To recap key events in the story
Time: 15–20 minutes
Organization: Give each student, or group of students a copy of the worksheet. Ask them to identify who said these words and who to. Encourage them also to discuss what the statements are about and how they fit into the story. When the students have finished, go through the answers as a class and generate discussion about how the different quotations fit into the plot.

Key: 1 Father to children, about broken train; 2 Mother to kids, about not having much money; 3 Station Master to Peter, about stealing coal; 4 Mother to children, about gift from old gentleman; 5 Phyllis to her brother and sister about landslide; 6 Perks to wife, about his birthday presents; 7 Old gentleman to Mother, about his visit; 8 Mother to Bobbie, about Father; 9 Jim to the children, about falling in the tunnel; 10 Perks to Bobbie, about her father's release from prison.

STAGE 3

Recycling
Sue Stewart

Introduction

Chapter summary

Chapter 1 (The rubbish problem) shows what rubbish is and what happens to it. Most people don't think about these questions but now we are producing too much rubbish and there are not enough places to put it. Rubbish is a problem for all countries, rich and poor alike.

Chapter 2 (5,000 years of rubbish and recycling) looks at the problem of rubbish as an old one. It began when people started living in towns. At first people just threw their rubbish into the streets. This meant that big cities became very dirty. The problem increased with the growth of factories. Workers were paid to take away rubbish from towns. People in poor countries still do this today, but it is dirty and dangerous work.

Chapter 3 (Our throwaway world) describes how in the past people kept things for a long time, but today things don't last as long. We live in a throwaway world. But there is an alternative: we can recycle things instead of throwing them away.

Chapter 4 (Glass and paper) shows how both glass and paper can be easily recycled. We can re-use glass bottles and use waste paper to make many things.

Chapter 5 (Metal and plastic) looks at how aluminium and steel can also be easily recycled. However, it is more difficult to recycle plastic and we throw away billions of plastic bags each year. These can harm and even kill animals when they eat them. Although it is possible to recycle some plastic, it would be better to use less plastic.

Chapter 6 (Other problems) concentrates on computers and mobile phones having changed people's lives. But people are always wanting to buy new phones and computers so what can be done with the old ones? They can be sent to people in poor countries. Other machines can be recycled too.

Chapter 7 (Paper houses and Everest bells) shows how beautiful things, such as bags, jewellery, and bowls, can be made from recycled materials. Many artists have used recycled materials in their work. And useful things can be made from recycled materials too: a Japanese architect has even made buildings from waste paper.

Chapter 8 (Recycling around the world) describes the different approaches to recycling in different countries. Germany and Switzerland recycle almost everything. Other countries have rewarded people for recycling. In Africa hardly anything is thrown away: everything can be used time and time again.

Chapter 9 (What can you do?) is about what ordinary people can do to tackle the problem of rubbish disposal. When you go shopping you can take your own bags instead of using the supermarket's. Buy from shops which don't use a lot of plastic packaging. Think of ways you can use old things again. And give your old boxes, cards, and magazines to schools. They can always make good use of them.

Chapter 10 (The future) looks to the future. There are many examples of communities all over the world supporting recycling projects. Freecycle is an organization which encourages people to exchange things they don't want for things they do. Even supermarkets are changing their thinking: many now offer customers bags which can be recycled instead of plastic bags. Perhaps the 21st century will see the end of our throwaway world.

Background

Some more facts and figures about recycling:

1) Taiwan has prohibited plastic bags and also plastic cutlery used in fast-food restaurants. As a result there has been a 25% reduction in landfill waste.

2) In Ireland a 15% tax on plastic bags has resulted in a 90% reduction in their use.

3) Up to 50% of rubbish in the average dustbin could be turned into compost.

4) The largest lake in Britain could we filled with unrecycled rubbish from Britain in eight months.

5) £36 million worth of aluminium is thrown away every year, yet aluminium cans can be recycled and ready to use in 6 weeks.

6) An average family in Britain uses 500 glass bottles and jars every year. Glass is 100% recyclable.

7) British people use 12.5 million tonnes of paper and cardboard every year.

8) It takes 24 trees to make one tonne of paper.

Recycling
Pre-reading activity

What do you know?

1 *What do you know about Recycling? Tick the correct statements:*
  a Recycling means using things again instead of just throwing them away. ☐
  b The problem of what to do with rubbish is not new. ☐
  c Recycling is only a problem in rich countries. ☐
  d Burning rubbish is as good as recycling it. ☐
  e It isn't easy to recycle things like glass and paper. ☐
  f It isn't easy to recycle most kinds of plastic. ☐
  g There is nothing that ordinary people can do to make the world cleaner. ☐

2 *Here are some words and phrases which are important when thinking about recycling. Match the words with the definitions.*

1 landfill site	a something that makes electricity for watches, radios, etc.
2 compost	b light metal used for making cans.
3 battery	c paper or plastic material which is put around things you buy in shops
4 aluminium	d place where rubbish is put
5 packaging	e material made from leaves and vegetables used to make plants grow

3 *Which of these statements do you agree with? Which do you disagree with? In each case, say why.*
  a There has always been rubbish and we have always got rid of it. There is plenty of room in the world for all the rubbish we use. We can easily make more landfill sites.
  b Everyone should be worried about rubbish. All of us can do something to recycle our rubbish. I'm going to make a compost heap in my garden and put all my leftover fruit and vegetables into it.
  c Recycling uses a lot of energy. Instead of recycling, we should be thinking about how we can use less paper, plastic, and glass.
  d I like new things. For example, there's a new phone this year which you can use to send emails. I want one!

To the teacher

Aim: To prepare students to read about the story of the USA
Time: 15–20 minutes
Organization: 1 Bring in some ordinary objects such as a glass bottle, a newspaper, a metal can, a plastic bag, an old radio, a wooden box, and ask students which of these things could be recycled. Which would be easiest to recycle, which most difficult? Then ask them to do Exercise 1 either individually or in pairs. Exercise 3 is meant to get students thinking about some of the important issues which are dealt with in *Recycling*. Although b and c reflect views that will be expressed in the book and a and

d go against these views, there should still be room for discussion of all these views. The aim of this exercise is to make students think about some of the issues that they will be reading about in the book. After they have read the book, ask them to look at these questions again. Have they changed their opinions about these statements?
Key 1: Students should tick Statements a, b, and f. Ask students to say why the other statements are wrong. The answers to c and d can be found in Chapter 1, e in Chapter 4, and g in Chapter 9.
Key 2: 1d, 2 e, 3 a, 4 b, 5c.

Recycling
While reading activity

Spot the mistakes

Read this summary of the first part of Chapter 3, Our throwaway world (up to the end of page 12), and correct the mistakes.

Recycling is a modern idea. Very rich people used to collect things that other people threw away and bought them. In the past there was as much rubbish as there is today. People kept things for a long time and then sold them to their children. Nowadays it is the same. People change things like cars and phones all the time. It is more difficult to buy new things than to have old things repaired. And people also want to be fashionable and have the oldest phone or TV. They like to have new things and they like to buy things which are expensively packaged. Sometimes the packaging is less important than what is inside. Toys are sometimes so badly packaged that children prefer the packaging to the toy!

Now write a summary of the second part of Chapter 3. Include four mistakes. When you have written it, give it to someone to correct.

_____

_____

_____

_____

_____

_____

To the teacher

Where: At the end of chapter 3
Time: 30 minutes
Aim: To get students to focus on how we have become a society which constantly wants new things
Organization: Make a copy of this worksheet for each student. Ask students to look at the summary and say what it's about. Go over the first mistake with the class. Then ask them to rewrite the summary correcting the remaining mistakes. Allow 10 minutes for this. Then ask students to write a summary of the second part of Chapter 3, that is, from the top of page 13. Remind them that they should include four mistakes. When students have written their summaries, ask them to swap them with their neighbours. Students correct the 'mistakes', as in the first part of the activity. Check the results with the whole class.

Key: The corrected summary should look like this:
Recycling is *not* a modern idea. Very poor people used to collect things that other people threw away and *sold* them. In the past there was *not* as much rubbish as there is today. People kept things for a long time and then *gave* them to their children. Nowadays it is *different*. People change things like cars and phones all the time. It is *easier* to buy new things than to have old things repaired. And people also want to be fashionable and have the *latest/oldest* phone or TV. They like to have new things and to buy things which are *nicely/beautifully* packaged. Sometimes the packaging is *more* important than what is inside. Toys are sometimes so well packaged that children prefer the packaging to the toy!

Recycling

After reading activity

What about you?

What do people in your town or country do about recycling? Find out the answer to these questions:

1 Do you have to take rubbish to a recycling point or is rubbish collected from your house?

2 If rubbish is collected, how often is it collected – daily, once a week, every two weeks?

3 Who pays for local rubbish collection? Is it the national or the local government? Does the money for recycling come from money people pay to the government in taxes?

4 Are there different bins for different materials – for example, plastic, glass, paper? How many different bins are there?

5 Do local shops give customers plastic bags for their shopping? Are they disposable or recyclable?

6 What does your town council do to make people more aware of the need to recycle?

7 Do local schools teach students about recycling? Are there recycling bins in or around the schools? Do students take part in recycling activities?

When you have collected this information, write (a letter, an email, a newspaper article) to the town council saying what you have found out about recycling in your town and making suggestions for what more could be done to improve it.

To the teacher

Aim: To get students to relate what they have learnt about recycling to their own lives by finding out what is being done about it in their own environment

Time: 30 minutes (Much longer if outside sources are consulted)

Organization: Think of this as a project. First students have to collect the information. Ask students to work in pairs or small groups. They may know some of the answers to the questions already: they may have to find out the answers to others. To save time, you may want to brainstorm the answers so that finally all students have the information they need to write.

Students can write in any format they like, but each group should decide which format they are going to use. What they write should be divided into two short paragraphs: what they have discovered about recycling in their town and what needs to be done to improve it now. You may want to give them a leading sentence for each paragraph, e.g.

We have discovered that in (name of town) recycling is done as follows…

We suggest that in future (name of town) should …

STAGE 3

The Secret Garden

Frances Hodgson Burnett

Introduction

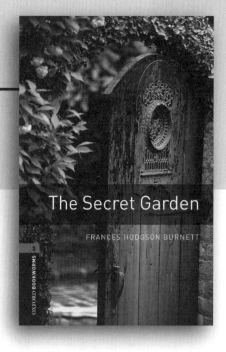

The story

Mary is born in India to rich parents who spend little time with her. Instead she is brought up by her Indian maid, Kamala, who does everything. Mary has a thin angry face and is selfish and disagreeable. One day, a terrible illness sweeps through the house, leaving both her parents dead. Mary is left alone and only finds out about their deaths by accident.

Mary is sent to England to live with her uncle, Mr Archibald Craven. She has never met him before but hears that he is a bad-tempered man with a crooked back, who lives in a large house in Yorkshire, in the north of England. Since the death of his lovely young wife ten years ago, he has spent his time alone.

When Mary arrives at the cold dark house she is rude and aggressive. However, one kind servant, Martha, is friendly to her. She explains that Mary's new life will be very different and she will now have to look after herself. Mary is miserable until Martha talks about her large family who are poor but happy. Mary is especially interested in her twelve year old brother, Dickon, who loves animals. Martha also tells Mary about a secret garden which has been locked since the death of Mrs Craven.

Mary finds the secret garden but cannot see the entrance. She meets the surly but kind gardener, Ben, who makes her realise how ugly and disagreeable she is. Ben introduces Mary to his only friend, a robin, who shows Mary the key and the hidden door to the garden, which she enters. It is the loveliest, most exciting place she has ever seen. She decides to restore the garden.

Mary is now much more agreeable and becomes friends with Martha, and Dickon who supplies her with seeds for the garden. She meets Mr Craven and decides that he is a kind but very unhappy man.

There is one thing that puzzles Mary. She sometimes hears the mysterious sound of crying but nobody else will admit they can hear it. One night she goes to a lonely bedroom where she finds Colin, Mr Craven's son, who she didn't know existed. Mr Craven doesn't see Colin because he is a reminder of his dead wife. A doctor has made Colin believe that he will die or grow up with a crooked back, so he spends all his time in bed and cannot walk. The doctor is Colin's uncle who will inherit money if Colin and his father die.

Colin and Mary become good friends and she tells him all about the secret garden. However, one day they have an argument. Mary shouts at Colin, looks at his back and declares there is nothing wrong with him. This is an important moment for Colin. Dickon and Mary secretly take Colin to the garden in his wheelchair. Colin stands up for the first time and eventually learns to walk.

Colin's father dreams one night that his wife is calling him to the garden. He returns to England and visits the garden for the first time in ten years. Colin runs towards him looking healthy, happy and strong. Father and son fall into each other's arms in the garden which has been restored to its former beauty.

Background to the story

Another children's story by Frances Hodgson Burnett (1849–1924), *A Little Princess*, is available in the Oxford Bookworms Series (see the Oxford Graded Readers Catalogue), although at a lower level.

Before reading

Here are some ways to help your students approach the story:

1 Give students the title of the book and show them the picture on the cover. Ask them to try and guess what kind of story it is.

2 Ask the students to read the text on the back cover of the book, and the story introduction on the first page. Then ask them a few questions about the story, or use the Before Reading Activities in the back of each Bookworm.

3 Use the pre-reading activity in this worksheet.

The Secret Garden
Pre-reading activity

Match the words with the pictures

a It was the loveliest, most exciting place Mary had ever seen.

b Just then Mrs Medlock appeared.

c Ben stopped smiling and picked up his spade.

d A boy ran out, a tall, healthy, handsome boy, straight into the man's arms.

e 'Who are you?' the boy whispered.

f Mary saw that there was a different Indian servant by her bed.

g Dickon pushed the wheelchair all round the garden.

h Mary's uncle had black hair with some white in it, and high, crooked shoulders.

To the teacher

Aim: To familiarize students with the setting and characters

Time: 15 minutes

Organization: Give a copy of the worksheet to each student or pair of students. Ask them to match the words with the pictures.

Key: 1e, 2d, 3a, 4f, 5b, 6c, 7h, 8g.

When they have done this ask them the following questions:

1 When is the story set?

2 Who are the different characters? How old are they?

3 Which picture comes nearest to the end of the story?

4 What happens in the story?

It is not important for students to get the correct answers, only to discuss their ideas about the story.

The Secret Garden

STAGE 3

While reading activity

What's he / she like?

	Mary	Martha	Dickon	Mr Craven	Colin	Mrs Medlock	Ben Weatherstaff
friendly							
happy							
sad							
rich							
poor							
selfish							
generous							
weak							
strong							
pretty							
handsome							
ugly							
bad-tempered							
charming							
wise							

To the teacher

Where: At the end of chapter 5

Aim: To revise characters and characteristics through discussion

Time: 25 minutes

Organization: Give each student, or group of students a copy of the grid. Check the meaning of any new vocabulary. Ask them to tick the adjectives which are relevant to the particular characters. Encourage plenty of discussion. Students may have slightly different answers but they must be able to justify their ideas.

STAGE 3

The Secret Garden

After reading activity

Who said what?

Complete the table.

		WHO?	WHO TO?	WHAT ABOUT?
1	'It's dangerous to stay in this town. You should go to the hills.'			
2	'He won't want to see you, so you must stay out of his way and do what you're told.'			
3	'My mother always says people should be able to take care of themsleves.'			
4	'We're not pretty to look at, and we're both very disagreeable.'			
5	'You didn't hear anything! Go back to your room now.'			
6	'I like you. I never thought I'd like as many as five people!'			
7	'All the servants have to do what I want, because if I'm angry, I become ill.'			
8	'There's nothing the matter with your horrid back!'			
9	'I wish – you were my mother!'			
10	'You can't believe it! I can't believe it myself.'			

To the teacher

Aim: To recap key events in the story
Time: 15–20 minutes
Organization: Give each student, or group of students a copy of the worksheet. Ask them to identify who said these words and who to. Encourage them also to discuss what the statements are about and how they fit into the story. When the students have finished, go through the answers as a class and generate discussion about how the different quotations fit into the plot.

Key: 1 Young man to Mary's mother, about the illness in India; 2 Mrs Medlock to Mary, about Mr Craven; 3 Martha to Mary, about getting dressed; 4 Ben Weatherstaff to Mary, about their characters; 5 Mrs Medlock to Mary, about the crying; 6 Mary to Dickon, about their friendship; 7 Colin to Mary, about his illness; 8 Mary to Colin, about his back; 9 Colin to Mrs Sowerby, about missing his dead mother; 10 Colin to his father, about walking.

Skyjack!

Tim Vicary

Introduction

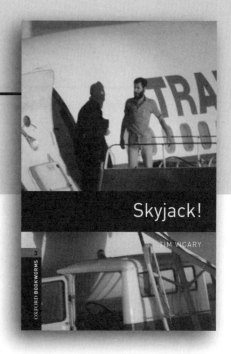

The story

A small group of terrorists hijack a plane with a number of passengers on board. The hijackers force the pilot to land at a small airport in the country they are flying over. They announce they are the People's Liberation Army, and threaten to hold the passengers hostage until certain demands are met. They ask the Government of the country to release two of their 'brothers', who were convicted of terrorist offences and are in prison not far away. The hijackers know that the Prime Minister is a woman, but at first they are not aware that her husband, Carl, is on the plane. His police bodyguard, Harald, makes a brave attempt to protect Carl, by pretending that Carl is a prisoner being escorted to another prison. Meanwhile, the Prime Minister, Helen Sandberg, meets police and military experts at the airport to discuss the situation. She asks the terrorists to set the hostages free, but the hijackers' reply is to shoot an American passenger in cold blood. They threaten to kill another passenger every half-hour until their fellow-terrorists are released. Helen orders the two convicted terrorists to be brought from prison to the airport. On the plane, Harald tries to overpower two of the hijackers, but fails. The terrorists identify Carl as the Prime Minister's husband, and are delighted, thinking she will agree to their demands to save her husband. In spite of pressure from the American and British Ambassadors, Helen and Colonel Carter, head of the commando unit, work out their own rescue plan. The hijackers agree that if one of the released prisoners is sent onto the plane, a hundred passengers will be freed. Then the plane will be refuelled, the other prisoner will reach the plane, and the other passengers will be set free. Only the pilot and Carl will be kept on the plane, to be freed later. In fact, however, the commandos attack the plane, all the terrorists are shot or arrested, and the passengers, including Carl and Harald, are released safe and sound.

Background to the story

Skyjack! is set in an imaginary country, whose Prime Minister is a woman. She does not want to allow Britain or the USA to set up military bases there, and she is also determined to solve the problem of the hijacking without the help of the British or American Ambassadors and their military forces.

Terrorism occurs when individuals or groups of people use terror or violent action to draw attention to their cause, and may involve hijacking, bomb attacks, assassination of public figures, etc. Most societies consider that a terrorist act is one of the very worst crimes, and the punishment is usually a lengthy prison sentence, or in some countries, the death penalty. In the country in this story, the two 'brother' terrorists had tried to put a bomb on a plane, and had been sent to prison for thirty years.

Difficult decisions need to be taken when a hijack takes place. The authorities are under intense pressure to act fast, and act effectively. They must try to get all the hostages released unharmed, but also arrest and punish the hijackers.

Skyjack!
Pre-reading activity

Match the words with the pictures

a Helen was talking to the Airport Police on the telephone.
b The Colonel put some grenades in the coat pocket.
c 'Free! You are free now, brother!'
d Harald tore the passport into pieces. Then he ate them!
e 'Welcome aboard, sir.'
f Carl could see the bearded hijacker from the light of the instruments.
g The air hostess had a machine gun in her hand.

To the teacher

Aim: To familiarize students with the setting and to predict the plot
Time: 30 minutes
Organization: Give one copy of the worksheet to each student or each pair or group of students. Ask the students to match the picture with the correct caption. Now ask students to discuss what is happening in the pictures and how the people involved are probably feeling. Ask students to put the pictures in a suitable order for telling a story. Groups should exchange their opinions and story ideas. (Do not tell any group that they are right or wrong about the actual plot of *Skyjack!*)
Key: 1e, 2g, 3a, 4d, 5f, 6c, 7b.

Skyjack!
While reading activity

Pyramid discussion

1 The airline is responsible for passengers' safety. It is the airline's fault if a hijack happens.

★ ★ ★ ★ ★ ★ ★

2 Governments should never give terrorists what they want.

★ ★ ★ ★ ★ ★ ★

3 Terrorists are freedom-fighters, who have to hijack planes and take other violent action, because it is the only way to get publicity for their cause.

★ ★ ★ ★ ★ ★ ★

4 The crew of the plane should carry guns and be able to fight off any hijackers.

★ ★ ★ ★ ★ ★ ★

5 It is not important if some passengers die, as long as the terrorists are caught and punished.

6 Passengers should not just accept the hijackers' orders; they should try to fight the terrorists.

★ ★ ★ ★ ★ ★ ★

7 Security in airports should be much stricter, to prevent hijacking.

★ ★ ★ ★ ★ ★ ★

8 Police can promise the hijackers anything, in order to get the passengers freed. Then the promises can be broken.

★ ★ ★ ★ ★ ★ ★

9 People who travel by air two or three times a year should expect to be hijacked sometime in their lives.

★ ★ ★ ★ ★ ★ ★

10 Hijackers should be given the death penalty.

To the teacher

Where: At the end of Chapter 9, or 10, or 11
Aim: To consider a variety of opinions on the theme of hijacking
Time: 50–60 minutes
Organization: Give each student a copy of the list of statements below, and ask them individually (1) to decide which ones they agree with and to rank them in order according to how strongly they feel. Then put students in pairs (2) to repeat the task and, after

discussion, produce an order based on compromise. Then put students in fours (4) to repeat the activity. Students repeat the activity in groups of eight (8) and so on until finally, the class can decide the preferred order together.

This activity gives students the opportunity to repeat their arguments, listen to new views, and try to persuade or dissuade, as the pyramid grows.

Skyjack!
After reading activity

Who said what, to whom, where and what about?

	WHO?	WHO TO?	WHERE?	WHAT ABOUT?
1 'We've been away for a long time.'				
2 'There is a change of plan.'				
3 'I'll look at it while you make me a cup of coffee.'				
4 'She will do what we say.'				
5 'This is going to be very difficult, isn't it?'				
6 'I won't let you die for me, you know.'				
7 'I can't bring them here.'				
8 'You're a murderer!'				
9 'They'll just take that goddam plane apart.'				
10 'I don't think you understand what you're doing.'				
11 'We will set them free later.'				
12 'I told you, this is a serious mistake.'				
13 'It was an expensive raincoat.'				
14 'Is it him? Yes, it is!'				
15 'You must not do that.'				
16 'I think we're in the news again.'				

To the teacher

Aim: To focus students' attention back on the characters
Time: 15–20 minutes

Organization: Give each student or group of students a copy of the chart below. Ask them to identify who said these words, who to, where and about what.

The Star Zoo

Harry Gilbert

Introduction

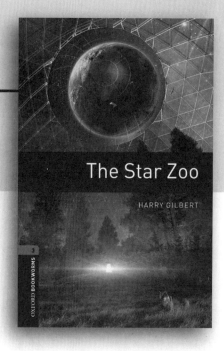

The Star Zoo

HARRY GILBERT

The story

Hummingbird (Hummy for short) lives in about 22,500 AD, on a planet a long way from Earth. None of the people who live in this time have ever seen an animal. All the animals were killed twenty thousand years before by the pollution on Earth, and people have spread out across the Galaxy – alone. They remember the animals in their names, and in the Book of Remembering.

Hummy is forced to marry Buffalo, a man she does not know and certainly does not love. She runs away in her family's robot spaceship, and by chance, discovers a big, old plastic spaceship. The spaceship is full of plants – and animals. At first, Hummy is horrified and wants to kill the animals. She does not want to share her Galaxy with other species. But soon she starts to get used to the idea. Hummy then meets the computer which controls the spaceship. The computer explains that the spaceship (which is made of old plastic bottles) is a Star Zoo which left Earth with the last surviving animals, twenty thousand years earlier.

Hummy returns to her planet with the news, but nobody believes her. She persuades Buffalo to return to the Star Zoo with her to prove she is telling the truth. But when they get there, the shock of seeing the animals turns Buffalo mad. Hummy is young enough to adapt to the idea of the animals, but it is impossible for someone older, like him.

Hummy does not know what to do – clearly if the animals send Buffalo mad, it's going to be very difficult to get other people to accept them. The computer suggests that she gets a robot to make robot animals. People might find robot animals less frightening, and this might help them to accept animals.

Hummy takes her spaceship, a robot, and a robot animal to New Earth, to show the robot animal to the Star Council. Even though it is only a robot, the robot animal has the same effect on the members of the Star Council as it did on Buffalo – it sends them crazy, and one of them shoots and destroys it.

Hummy has to stay on New Earth, because it is decided that nobody must know about the Star Zoo – they might want to destroy it. She is given a job looking after some young children. After a time, she realises that it might be safe for young children to see an animal. The robot, it appears, had made two robot animals, so the children get to meet the second one – and it is a success. Hummy realises that people can learn to live with animals, provided they start when they are very young.

Background to the story

The story links two very topical themes. Firstly, it takes the idea of global warming. Pollution leads to an increase in temperature which kills animals and forces humans to emigrate. Secondly, it looks at the problem of the survival of animal species. In our world, species of plants and animals dies out every month, and we have to find some way of protecting them. The Star Zoo, built out of recycled plastic bottles and operated by a second-hand computer takes the idea just a little further.

Before reading

Here are some ways to help your students approach the story:

1   Give students the title of the book and show them the picture on the cover. Ask them to try and guess what kind of the story it is.
2   Give students a copy of the text on the back cover of the book, and of the story introduction on the first page. When they have read the texts, ask them a few questions about the story, or use the Before Reading Activities in the back of each Bookworm.
3   Use the pre-reading activity in this worksheet.
4   If there is a recording of this title, play the first few pages and stop at an interesting point.

The Star Zoo
Pre-reading activity

Match the words with the pictures

a There was a sudden bright light. The little animal exploded. It was gone.

b First the robot made a plastic body which it covered with soft plastic, like a skin.

c But the thing had teeth – a mouth full of yellow, shiny teeth.

d I pulled and pushed and hit the big round door.

e The last dance began. You hold hands in a big circle round the fire – everybody together.

f I saw a spaceship land near the house. 'Who's coming?' I asked.

g These children were more trouble than any animal in the Star Zoo!

h Buff's face was full of hate and he was holding a laser gun.

To the teacher

Aim: To familiarize students with the story and its setting

Time: 10–15 minutes

Organization: Give one copy of the worksheet to each student or each group of students. Ask them to match the words with the appropriate picture. When the students have completed this task, check the answers with them. Then ask them to try and put the pictures into the order they might appear in the story. Students need only suggest an order which makes sense of the pictures.

Key: 1h, 2g, 3e, 4c, 5b, 6a, 7d, 8f.

The Star Zoo

While reading activity

What will happen next?

Which of these things do you think will happen in Chapter 7?

	WILL HAPPEN	MAY HAPPEN	WON'T HAPPEN	YOUR OWN COMMENTS
Buff shoots and kills Hoo-Woo.				
Hoo-Woo jumps and kills Buff before he manages to shoot.				
Hummy stops Buff shooting and persuades him to make friends with the animals.				
Buff doesn't kill Hoo-Woo, but he goes crazy.				
The animals push Buff out of the Star Zoo and make him return to Just Like Home.				

Which of these things do you think will happen in Chapter 10?

	WILL HAPPEN	MAY HAPPEN	WON'T HAPPEN	YOUR OWN COMMENTS
Hummy returns to Just Like Home.				
Hummy is put in prison.				
Hummy is killed because she is responsible for the death of some members of the Star Council.				
Hummy returns to the Star Zoo and lives there for the rest of her life.				
Hummy finds a way of bringing animals to New Earth.				
Hummy becomes President of the Star Council.				

To the teacher

Where: At the end of Chapter 6 and at the end of Chapter 9

Aim: To encourage students to predict the development of the story

Time: 10 minutes

Organization: Give each student, or group of students, a copy of the first part of the worksheet. Ask them to discuss in groups and decide, without looking beyond the end of Chapter 6, what will happen as the story unfolds. It is not important whether their predictions are correct, although it may be interesting for students to keep their worksheets and see whether or not they were right. At the end of Chapter 9 students should do the same with the second part of the worksheet.

The Star Zoo
After reading activity

Someone else's story

Complete the paragraphs about each character.

BUFFALO

I wanted to marry Hummy the first time I saw her, and I was very pleased when I found her from the photograph I took of her eyes.
But ....
....
....
....
....

COMPUTER

I waited for fifteen thousand years, so I was very, very happy when ....
....
....
....
....
....

HUMMIE'S FATHER

Hummingbird was not usually a difficult daughter, and I was very surprised when she said she ran away. When she came back
....
....
....
....
....
....
....
....
....

THE OLD STAR COUNCILLOR

I was very lucky that I wasn't in the room when the other Councillors saw the robot animal. I ....
....
....
....
....
....
....
....
....

To the teacher

Aim: To encourage students to retell the story from the point of view of some of the other characters
Time: 45–60 minutes or more

Organization: Give each student a copy of the worksheet. Ask them to think about the story from the point of view of some of the other characters, and then write a continuation of the story from the prompts given.

Tales of Mystery and Imagination

Edgar Allan Poe

Introduction

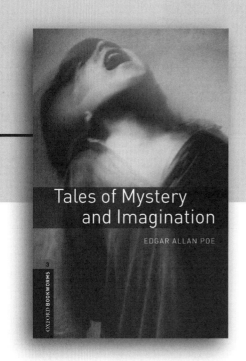

Tales of Mystery and Imagination

EDGAR ALLAN POE

OXFORD BOOKWORMS

3

The stories

The Fall of the House of Usher. The story begins with the narrator arriving at the house of his friend, Roderick Usher, who is both physically and mentally ill. From the outside the house is very gloomy and full of cracks and holes; on the inside there are shadows everywhere. Roderick's sister, Lady Usher, is slowly dying and Roderick fears both her death, and the presence of fear itself. Lady Usher is buried, while in a trance, but two weeks later escapes from her coffin, bursts into the room and dies. The narrator rushes from the house which then collapses to the ground.

The Black Cat. The narrator explains that he has always loved animals. His and his wife's house was full of pets. When he turned to drink, the narrator was cruel to his animals and eventually hanged the favourite cat, Pluto. Later, after the house had burned down and while trying to kill his new cat, he killed his wife instead. He hid the body behind a wall in the cellar. When the police came, they heard a cat behind the wall and found the cat and the body of the narrator's wife.

The Masque of the Red Death. In this tale, a country is troubled by a terrible disease called the Red Death, which leaves blood on the body and face of its victims. Prince Prospero refuses to be troubled by the Red Death and invites a thousand friends to live a life of pleasure and amusement. At the end of five months he holds a masked ball, in splendid rooms designed and furnished mysteriously, lit only by fires. All the guests are dressed like a terrible dream, but one figure, dressed like Death, strikes fear into everyone's hearts. The prince becomes angry and attacks this figure with his sword. The prince dies and the guests discover the figure is Death and die.

William Wilson. As he waits for his own execution, the narrator tells us the story of his evil life.

For most of his life he has been shadowed by his double (*Doppelganger*) who first appeared at school, bearing the same name and identical mannerisms. At various stages in his life at school and after, the double interfered in William Wilson's plans when they were particularly dangerous and evil. William Wilson was a man who liked gambling, drinking, and other vices. He was forced to leave the University of Oxford when his card cheating was revealed by his double. Finally, furious at being prevented from seducing the wife of another man, the narrator killed his double.

The Tell-Tale Heart. This is another story related by a mad narrator who has very sensitive hearing and an intense dislike of the blue eyes of the old man who lives with him. He decides to kill the old man: each night for over a week, he gradually enters the room and shines his lantern onto the old man but the eyes are closed. On the eighth night, the old man is awake and terrified when the narrator finally kills him to stop the neighbours hearing the sound of the old man's beating heart. The narrator carefully cuts the body up and hides it under the floor boards so when the police arrive he is confident. But later the narrator is sure they can hear the sound of the old man's heart and tears the floor boards up in front of the police.

Background to the stories

The poet and short-story writer Edgar Allan Poe was born in 1809 in Boston, Massachussetts. He joined the army at the end of his first year at the University of Virginia to pay for his gambling debts. This was followed by a spell in the navy before he was dishonourably discharged for intentionally neglecting his duty. He concentrated on writing and became famous for his short story *The Fall of the House of Usher*, and the poem *The Raven*. Fame, however, did not bring him security, and he struggled with alcholism, nervous anxiety and poverty until his tragic death in 1849, after lying semi-conscious and delirious for five days.

Tales of Mystery and Imagination
Pre-reading activity

Every picture tells a story

The Fall of the House of Usher

- -

The Black Cat

- -

The Masque of the Red Death

- -

William Wilson

- -

The Tell-Tale Heart

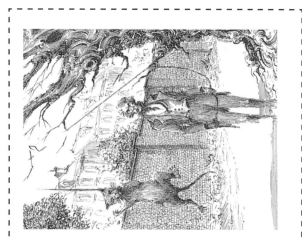

To the teacher

Aim: To perceive connection of details and clues found in visual information usually accompanying text

Time: 30–45 minutes

Organization: First, photocopy the illustrations above and on the next page, which are taken from the book, and mount them on card. Then write or stick the five story titles on separate pieces of card, as shown. Now, divide the class into groups, and make sure that each group has a full set of ten illustration cards and five story-title cards. Ask them to decide which two illustrations they think belong to which story title. (Some will be easier than others, but do not tell students if they have made the right choice.) Write the following questions on the board and ask the students to discuss them and make suggestions.

One student in each group can act as secretary and write down the suggestions.

1 What, if anything, seems to be happening in each picture?

2 What kinds of feelings are suggested by the pictures – fear, sadness, enjoyment, gloom, horror, excitement, pleasure, terror, happiness?

3 What caption can you suggest to go with each picture? If there is a character in the picture, it might be a speech bubble or a thought bubble for that person.

4 Suggest briefly what you think each story might be about.

When you are sure that each group is clear about its ideas, then the groups can exchange their theories and opinions.

Tales of Mystery and Imagination

While reading activity

Happy adjectives and friendly nouns

ADJECTIVES	NOUNS
deep	*gloom*
happy	*thought*
dark	
large	*house*
strange	*lake*
sad	
mysterious	*water*
heavy	*letter*
pale	
thin	*family*
soft	*fear*
ghostly	
silent	*cloud*
fantastic	*face*
terrible	
wild	*hair*
calm	*light*
friendly	
honest	*story*
violent	*cat*
huge	
horrible	*dream*
peaceful	*sleep*
loud	
evil	*scream*

To the teacher

Aim: To explore the various meanings of adjectives in a collocation matching game

Time: 20 minutes

Organization: Show the list above on the board or on an overhead projector, or provide photocopied sheets. Divide the class into groups and tell them they have ten minutes to write down as many possible adjective-and-noun combinations as they can.

Tell them they can pick unusual combinations, but they must be able to justify or explain them afterwards. For example, can you have 'horrible water' (yes, if it is drinking water and has a bad taste, or smells of fish), or 'a silent scream' (perhaps you can have one in a dream)? When the ten minutes is over, each group in turn says how many combinations it has got and reads them out. The other groups judge if the combination is acceptable. If they don't like the combination, they can ask for explanations and then take a vote on whether to allow it. The winning group is the one with the highest number of acceptable combinations.

Read all about it!

The Rich and the Cruel punished at last.

Strange deaths of brother and sister.

Is this the most evil man in Europe?

Man hears voice of Hell.

To the teacher

Aim: To interpret events and to write accounts in role
Time: 60–90 minutes
Organization: For this activity, students can imagine that they work for a sensationalist newspaper. They will produce a front page which contains articles describing the events in each of the stories in the book. They can therefore employ all the journalistic tactics necessary, such as additions to the story, interpretation of events, speculation of motive/outcome, and witness interviews.

Prepare a skeletal front page by dividing the space to accommodate the five stories. Prepare titles for each of the stories and set them out on the front page. The headlines above may be used.

In class, ask the students to decide which story is being referred to by which headline, and which characters may be interviewed in connection with each event. Then ask them to suggest generally what they would expect to read in each news item, and which part of the story would receive most attention. Try to establish how journalists might feel about each event – would they be shocked, horrified, pleased, afraid?

Divide the students into five groups and allocate a story to each group. Remind them of the journalistic tactics mentioned above, and the fact that journalists have a way of building big stories out of very little information.

A second copy of the front page should be made. From this copy each individual story shape should be cut out. In each group appoint a sub-editor who has responsibility for checking grammar and spelling.

Make sure that each group has prepared notes on the 'angle' of their story and which witnesses to interview. For example, in *The Tell-Tale Heart*, perhaps the old man who was murdered talked to a neighbour before he died and described how afraid he was of the strange young man in his house. The journalist could then interview the neighbour and one of the arresting policemen. In this way, you can encourage students to make 'their' story the most horrible or the most shocking. They cannot alter anything that happened in their story, but they can extend or enhance it.

Each sub-editor, when happy with the story, gives it to the Editor (teacher) who does any final checking. The stories are then glued into position on the second copy of the front page, which can then be displayed or circulated for the students to keep.

STAGE 3

The Three Strangers And Other Stories

Thomas Hardy

Introduction

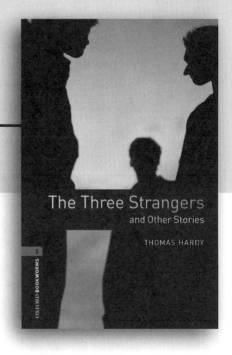

> *This ungraded summary is for the teacher's use only and should not be given to students.*

The Stories

The Three Strangers. It is a cold, wet, night in the hills and Shepherd Fennel and his wife are having a party to celebrate the birth of a new baby. In the middle of the party there is a knock on the door and a stranger asks if he can shelter a while from the rain. He sits in the corner of the room, by the fire. A short while later a second stranger arrives, and he, too, asks for shelter. He joins the first stranger by the fire. The second man tells the people in the cottage that he is the hangman, and they realise that he is on his way to the nearby town, where he will hang a man for stealing a sheep. Then there is a third knock on the door, but this time the third stranger sees the two other strangers by the fire and runs off into the night. Then a gun is heard in the distance and they all realise that a prisoner has escaped from the prison and that this was probably the third stranger. The hangman organizes a chase, and then returns to the cottage, says goodbye to the first stranger and the two men walk off in different directions. When the shepherds finally catch the third stranger they realise that he is not the prisoner but his brother – the prisoner was the first man. He is never recaptured.

What the Shepherd Saw. In the middle of the night, in the empty hills, a shepherd boy watches a man meeting and embracing a woman. The next night the man returns, and the boy sees the woman's husband, the Duke, kill him and hide the body. The Duke discovers that the boy saw the murder of the man he thought was his wife's lover, and in exchange for the boy's silence he takes him into his house and gives him an education. The boy keeps the secret until after the Duke has died.

A Moment of Madness. Baptista is to marry an older man, her father's best friend. Although she doesn't dislike the man, she certainly isn't in love with him. A few days before the wedding is due, she meets Charles, a friend from college. He asks her to marry him and she agrees. Within two days they are married, but on the afternoon of their wedding Charles goes swimming in the sea and is drowned. Baptista

decides that the best thing to do is to keep this all secret and go ahead with the wedding to the older man. Some time after their wedding, circumstances force Baptista to tell the whole story to her new husband. He is not angry – he is relieved – for he, too, has a secret. He has married Baptista because he has four secret daughters that he wants her to look after, and Baptista has to welcome the girls into her home. But, surprisingly, she grows to love both the girls and her older husband.

Background to the stories

The stories, like all of Hardy's, are set in the south of England. The first two stories, *The Three Strangers* and *What the Shepherd Saw*, seem to be set at the beginning of the nineteenth century, when laws were harsh and ordinary people could not stand up to the aristocracy. The third story, *A Moment of Madness*, is set at the end of the nineteenth century at a time when women like Baptista were beginning to go out to work.

Before reading

Here are some ways to help your students approach the story:

1 Give students the title of the book and show them the picture on the cover. Ask them to try and guess what kind of story it is.

2 Ask the students to read the text on the back cover of the book, and the story introduction on the first page. Then ask them a few questions about the story, or use the Before Reading Activities in the back of each Bookworm.

3 Use the pre-reading activity in this worksheet.

4 If there is a recording of this title, play the first few pages and stop at an interesting point.

The Three Strangers and Other Stories

Pre-reading activity

People, places, and things

There are three stories in this book. Look at the sentences and decide which of the three stories they belong to.

	THE THREE STRANGERS	WHAT THE SHEPHERD SAW	A MOMENT OF MADNESS
a A boy sees a murder.			
b Three people come to a cottage in the night.			
c A boy and an old man look after some sheep.			
d A woman marries very suddenly.			
e Two men sit by the fire drinking.			
f A shepherd invites some men he doesn't know into his cottage.			
g A man goes swimming in the sea.			
h A man keeps a horrible secret for many years.			
i A woman keeps a secret from her husband.			
j A man runs away into the night.			
k A poor boy becomes rich.			
l A woman misses a boat and her life changes.			

To the teacher

Aim: To familiarize students with the setting and think about the possible themes of the stories

Time: 10–20 minutes

Organization: Give one copy of the worksheet to each student or each group of students. Check through the words and explain any unknown meanings. Alternatively, the students could look up any difficult words in their dictionaries. Then ask the students to work through the sentences, deciding which ones would be true for which story – make it clear that it does not matter if they are right or wrong. Give no indication as to whether the students have guessed correctly or not.

Key: The Three Strangers: b, e, f, j. What the Shepherd Saw: a, c, h, k. A Moment of Madness: d, g, i, l.

The Three Strangers and Other Stories

After reading activity

Problem letters

Look at these parts of letters from people in one of the stories. Which story is it and who are they from?

a I'm sorry that I didn't come back the second night but I couldn't

b I must see you. Can you come up onto the hills in the night?

c nobody know that I saw there, not even the boy, and I have told nobody

d now I am a rich man, but I can never forget

Now write extracts from three or four more letters from people in one of the other stories.

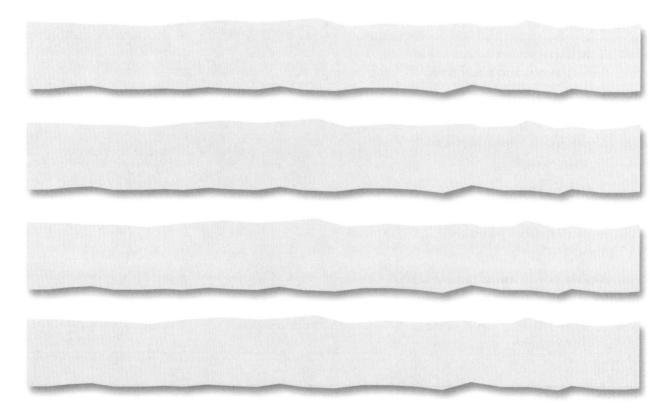

To the teacher

Aim: To focus students' attention back on the characters

Time: 10–20 minutes

Organization: Give one copy of the worksheet to each student or each group of students. Ask them to read the extracts and decide which story they are from and who wrote them. Then ask them to write similar extracts for one of the other stories – they can give these to other students to answer.

Key: The letters are from What the Shepherd Saw and are from the Duchess, Fred, the old shepherd, and Bill.

Through the Looking-Glass

Lewis Carroll

Introduction

The story

Alice steps through the Looking-glass and finds herself in a world that seems to be a giant chess game and where everything happens backwards. Once she starts to explore, many strange things happen to her. First, she finds herself in a large flower garden where the flowers speak to her. There, she meets the Red Queen who tells her she can be part of the chess game. She can begin by being a White Pawn and when she reaches the Eighth Square she will then become a Queen.

Alice has many adventures on her way to the Eighth Square. She goes on a train ride where she meets a man dressed in white paper, a goat, a beetle and a horse. In the wood where things have no name, she meets Tweedledum and Tweedledee, two identical brothers. Tweedledee reads her a poem called 'The Walrus and the Carpenter' and shows her the Red King who is asleep and snoring loudly. They tell her that she is not real; that she is only something in the king's dream and that if he wakes up she will disappear.

After that, she meets the White Queen who explains how everything happens backwards in this world. The next character she meets is Humpty Dumpty who tells her about 'unbirthday presents', presents you get when it's not your birthday. After that, she meets the Unicorn and the Lion who are fighting over the White King's crown. They stop fighting for a while and have a strange and magical tea party where the cake cuts itself.

Alice is shown the way to the Eighth Square by the White Knight whom she has witnessed having a battle with the Red Knight. Both are very bad at fighting and keep falling off their horses. Finally, she reaches the Eighth Square and becomes Queen. At a party to celebrate her becoming Queen, it becomes noisier and noisier, with food talking and cutlery dancing. Alice finally has enough, and pulls the tablecloth off the table in one swift move. This brings everything crashing to the ground and ends the dream.

Background to the story

Although Lewis Carroll was a mathematician and lectured at Christ Church College, Oxford, for over forty years, he is perhaps, best known for his children's books and poems. He was fascinated by the limits and paradoxes of language which he explored in his writing, perhaps most notably in his famous verse *Jabberwocky*. It is said that the popularity of his work stems from an interest in the many profound psychological perceptions evident in his writing and the mathematical logic underlying the fantasies. Even in his choice of pen name, this love of word play and logic is evident. He created his pen name by taking his names Charles Lutwidge, translating them into Latin as Carolus Ludovicus, reversing them to Ludovicus Carolus and finally translating them back into English as Lewis Carroll.

Before reading

Here are some ways to help your students approach the story:

1 Give students the title of the book and show them the picture on the cover. Ask them to try and guess what kind of story it is.

2 Ask the students to read the text on the back cover of the book, and the story introduction on the first page. Then ask them a few questions about the story, or use the Before Reading Activities in the back of each Bookworm.

3 Use the pre-reading activity in this worksheet.

4 If there is a recording of this title, play the first few pages and stop at an interesting point.

Through the Looking-Glass
Pre-reading activity

Match the words with the pictures

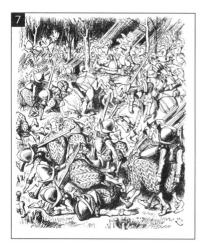

a Alice pinned up the Queen's hair more tidily.

b 'What is this on my head?' Alice said.

c 'It's just like a large chess-board!' Alice said.

d They were always falling over something or other.

e 'My name is Alice –'.

f In a moment the two Queens were both asleep, and snoring loudly.

g Alice got behind a tree, where she could watch more safely.

h 'Faster! Faster!' cried the Queen.

To the teacher

Aim: To familiarize students with the story and its setting

Time: 10–15 minutes

Organization: Give one copy of the worksheet to each student, or to each group of students. Ask them to match the pictures with the correct captions. When they have done this check the answers. Ask the students to answer these questions.

1 What kind of story is it?

2 In what kind of place does the story take place? Then ask them to put the pictures in the order they might appear in the story and to predict what the story might be. Tell them that there is no right or wrong answer to the activity.

Key: 1e, 2h, 3f, 4a, 5g, 6c, 7d, 8b.

Through the Looking-Glass

While reading activity

Word grid

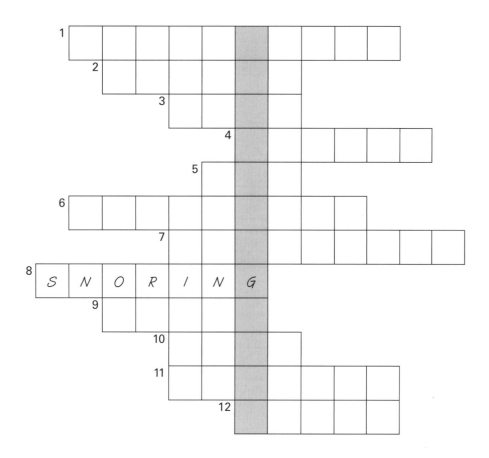

8 S N O R I N G

1 Tweedledee's friend.
2 A chess piece.
3 The place where things have no name.
4 Alice's pet.
5 The number of brooks in the Looking-Glass world.
6 One of the characters in Tweedledee's poem.
7 A talking flower.

8 Something the Red King is doing in chapter 4.
9 This belongs to the White Queen.
10 One of Alice's travelling companions on the train journey.
11 They were eaten by the Walrus and the Carpenter.
12 The shopkeeper in chapter 5.

To the teacher

Where: At the end of Chapter 5
Aim: To help clarify some key characters and events
Time: 20 minutes
Organization: Give one copy of the worksheet to each student, or to each group of students. Ask the students to read the clues and find the other missing words. When they have done all the questions they will find the central word in the grid which is *looking-glass*. When everyone has finished, go through the answers as a class. Ask them to give you another word for *looking-glass* and discuss its significance to the story with the class as a whole. Then ask them to discuss some of the characters. For example: Who were Tweedledum and Tweedledee? What did they look like? What was unusual about them?

Key: 1 Tweedledum, 2 bishop, 3 wood, 4 kitten, 5 six, 6 carpenter, 7 Tigerlily, 8 snoring, 9 shawl, 10 goat, 11 oysters, 12 sheep.

Through the Looking-Glass

After reading activity

Order the events

	EVENT	ORDER
a	Alice meets Tweedledum and Tweedledee.	
b	Alice reaches the Eighth Square and becomes a Queen.	
c	The White Queen cuts her finger.	
d	Humpty Dumpty reads Alice a poem.	
e	A Tiger-lily talks to Alice.	
f	The White Knight sings a song for Alice.	
g	Alice and the Red Queen run as fast as they can to keep still.	
h	Alice wakes up from the dream.	
i	The plum cake cuts itself into three pieces.	
j	The Red Queen introduces the pudding to Alice.	
k	Alice sees the Red King, the Red Queen, two Castles, two Pawns and a Bishop for the first time.	*1*
l	Alice meets the Lion and the Unicorn.	
m	Alice goes on a train journey.	
n	Tweedledee reads Alice a poem.	
o	Alice finds and opens a book and reads a poem called *Jabberwocky*.	
p	Alice pulls the tablecloth off the table at the tea party.	
q	The Red and White Knights fight for Alice.	
r	Alice buys an egg.	
s	The King's Messenger Haigha brings the King a message.	
t	Alice finds the wood where things have no name.	

To the teacher

Where: At the end of the book
Aim: To revise key events in the story
Time: 20–25 minutes
Organization: Give out copies of the worksheet.
Ask the students to put the sentences in the correct order as they appear in the story. When they have completed the task, check the answers with the class as a whole. Ask them to tell the story in pairs or in a round, adding details and expanding the storyline as they go.

Key: 1k, 2o, 3e, 4g, 5m, 6t, 7a, 8n, 9c, 10r, 11d, 12s, 13l, 14i, 15q, 16f, 17b, 18j, 19p, 20h.

Tooth and Claw – Short Stories

Saki

Introduction

The stories

Sredni Vashtar. Conradin is ten years old. His parents are dead, and he lives with an aunt who dislikes him. He lives a dull life, enriched by his imagination. At the bottom of the garden of his aunt's house, there is a shed, in which Conradin secretly keeps two animals – a chicken, and, in a large box, a ferret.

Conradin calls the ferret Sredni Vashtar and it becomes his god.

One day, his aunt discovers the chicken, and sells it. She also finds the ferret's box, and searches Conradin's room until she finds the key. While she goes down the garden to investigate, Conradin prays to his god.

His aunt does not come out of the shed, but Sredni Vashtar does, with blood on its neck and mouth. Conradin listens calmly, while the cook and housekeeper discover his aunt's body.

The Story-Teller. Three small children and their aunt are travelling in a train. Sitting near them is a bachelor, who is travelling alone. The children are getting bored, and although the aunt tries telling them a story, it is a boring story about a well-behaved little girl.

The bachelor is getting tired of the children's behaviour, so he offers to tell them a story. It is about a horribly good little girl, Bertha, who is so good that she has won three medals; the 'Never Late' medal, the 'Politeness' medal and the 'Best Child in the World' medal. The medals are enormous and clink when she walks.

Because she is such a good girl, the king allows her to walk in his palace gardens. Unfortunately, one day, a wolf comes into the gardens. Bertha manages to hide, but the clinking of the medals gives her away, and the wolf eats her.

The three children, of course, love this story.

Gabriel-Ernest. Van Cheele lives in the country, and one day he goes for a walk in the woods near his house. He meets a boy of about sixteen, naked beside a pool. The boy tells him he lives in the woods, eating rabbits, birds, chickens and – children.

The next day, Van Cheele finds the boy in his sitting-room. Van Cheele's aunt wants to help the boy, and gives him the name Gabriel-Ernest. Van Cheele is going to London for the day, and his aunt is giving a children's party. Gabriel-Ernest will help her. But when Van Cheele gets back home, his aunt tells him that Gabriel-Ernest is taking one of the children home after the party. Neither Gabriel-Ernest nor the boy are ever seen again, and Van Cheele realises that Gabriel-Ernest must be a werewolf.

Tobermory. Cornelius Appin manages to teach a cat, Tobermory, how to speak. But the experiment is not a success, as the cat listens to everybody's conversations and reports them to other people. And what will happen if Tobermory teaches other cats to speak? Finally, Tobermory, and one other cat who he has taught have to be killed.

A few weeks after that, Appin is killed by an elephant at Dresden Zoo. Perhaps he was trying to teach it to speak.

The She-Wolf. Leonard Bilsiter bores his friends with his stories of Siberian Magic, and his ability to turn people into animals. One day, Clovis Sangrail has had enough, and decides to trick Leonard. He borrows a very quiet, friendly wolf from a friend who has a private zoo, and arranges with Mrs Hampton that she will walk into the conservatory after dinner – and the wolf will appear.

Everybody is tricked, including poor Leonard Bilsiter, who the others think is responsible. Then Clovis reveals that he, too, can perform Siberian Magic – and Mrs Hampton reappears.

Tooth and Claw – Short Stories

Pre-reading activity

Word search

M	A	C	A	W	W	P	C	B	U	S	H	R	M	A	G	I	C	G	Y
E	A	L	V	V	U	P	Z	G	L	H	C	S	I	U	X	Y	I	R	T
M	R	A	Q	U	X	O	O	H	J	E	C	L	I	N	K	W	I	O	M
O	W	W	E	R	E	W	O	L	F	D	P	I	G	T	Q	U	I	W	I
R	A	B	B	I	T	E	B	K	E	L	E	P	H	A	N	T	B	L	L
I	Z	C	F	K	T	R	U	U	R	P	O	I	S	O	N	O	K	T	L
A	I	M	P	R	O	P	E	R	R	P	G	J	M	C	J	O	K	E	E
L	W	M	N	R	M	N	G	U	E	S	T	W	V	D	H	T	I	J	R
M	I	F	F	D	E	V	Z	T	T	G	O	D	L	B	M	H	N	X	S
F	O	R	B	I	D	D	E	N	W	L	A	K	O	F	R	Y	G	F	S
K	G	J	O	O	A	Y	J	C	O	N	S	E	R	V	A	T	O	R	Y
B	A	C	H	E	L	O	R	H	U	N	T	Q	D	G	S	T	A	I	N

To the teacher

Aim: To familiarize students with some of the key vocabulary and introduce the story

Time: 10–15 minutes

Organization: Give one copy of the wordsearch to each of the students (or each group of students) and ask them to try and identify some of the words. When they have found all, or most of the words check that they understand the meaning. Then ask

what sort of stories might contain these words (they also appear in the glossary).

Key: aunt, bachelor, bush, claw, clink, conservatory, elephant, ferret, forbidden, god, growl, guest, hunt, improper, joke, king, lord, macaw, magic, medal, memorial, miller, pig, poison, power, rabbit, shed, slip, stain, toast, tooth, werewolf, zoo.

Tooth and Claw – Short Stories

While reading activity

What will happen next?

Which of these things do you think will happen in the story? At the end of page 5.

	WILL HAPPEN	MAY HAPPEN	WON'T HAPPEN	YOUR OWN COMMENTS
Conradin's aunt will kill Sredni Vashtar.				
Sredni Vashtar will escape.				
Sredni Vashtar will kill Conradin's aunt.				
Sredni Vashtar has disappeared.				
Sredni Vashtar will bite Conradin's aunt.				
(Your own idea)				

At the end of page 39.

	WILL HAPPEN	MAY HAPPEN	WON'T HAPPEN	YOUR OWN COMMENTS
They discover that it is Mr Appin who is talking, not Tobermory.				
Tobermory teaches other cats to talk.				
They decide to kill Tobermory.				
Tobermory becomes the owner of the house.				
Mr Appin is killed.				
(Your own idea)				

To the teacher

Where: At the end of page 5 and at the end of page 39

Aim: To encourage students to predict the development of the story

Time: 5–10 minutes on two different occasions

Organization: Give each student, or group of students, a copy of the worksheet. Ask them to discuss in groups and decide, without looking beyond the end of page 5, what will happen to each of the three main characters. It is not important whether their predictions are correct, although it may be interesting for students to keep their worksheets and see whether or not they were right.

Tooth and Claw – Short Stories
After reading activity

Spot the mistakes

Sredni Vashtar

Conradin was a happy boy who loved to run and play football. He lived with his mother in a big, comfortable house with a garden. In the garden was a big shed, and Conradin had two animals in it – a black cat and a ferret. The ferret lived in a box, and Conradin brought it food every day. He prayed to the cat and asked it to make his aunt ill. She was ill for five days, and Conradin believed the cat had made her ill.

The next day, his aunt killed the cat. Then she asked Conradin for the key to the ferret's box, and Conradin gave it to her. She went down the garden and into the shed. When she opened the box, the ferret jumped out and killed her. Then it went back into its box. Conradin was having his tea. He looked out of the window and saw his aunt die. Then he went back inside the house and made himself another cup of tea.

Now write your summary here. Include at least ten mistakes.

....
....
....
....
....
....
....
....
....
....
....

To the teacher

Aim: To help students with summary writing
Time: 20–30 minutes
Organization: Give each student, or group of students, a copy of the worksheet. Ask them to correct the summary to Sredni Vashtar. The students should then write an erroneous summary of another story in the collection for another student, or group of students, to correct.

The USA

Alison Baxter

Introduction

Chapter summary

Chapter 1 (In the beginning) shows the USA as a vast country of more than 300 million people of all different races and ethnic groups.

Chapter 2 (The Pilgrim Fathers) looks at how Christopher Columbus reached the New World in 1492, but it was not until the 17th century that Europeans settled in America. The first of these were the Pilgrim Fathers. At first life was hard for them, but they learned much from the Native Americans.

Chapter 3 (The War of Independence) shows that by 1770 there were thirteen British colonies along the east coast of North America. But the colonists wanted to be free from British rule. They won the War of Independence and elected George Washington as their first president.

Chapter 4 (The Civil War) describes how the country kept on growing, and by the mid-19th century it had more than 31 million inhabitants. But there was conflict between the Northern and Southern states. The South wanted the right to keep its slaves, but President Lincoln opposed this. A bloody civil war between the North and the South ended with defeat for the South.

Chapter 5 (The Wild West) is about the 19th century and the USA moving west. Cowboys worked with cattle and drove them up to the North to be killed. Farmers moved west too and soon there was a railway from coast to coast.

Chapter 6 (Native Americans) shows that when the first Europeans landed in America, there were about two million Native Americans living there. But as white settlers moved west, they fought the Native Americans for their land. After their defeat at the battle of Wounded Knee, most Native Americans had to live in reservations.

Chapter 7 (New Americans) looks at the time between 1880 and 1930 when 27 million people emigrated from Europe to the USA. They were often poor and had suffered badly in their own countries.

Chapter 8 (Black Americans) shows that more than 10% of Americans today are black, the descendants of slaves brought to America from Africa. Although black slaves were set free after the Civil War, they suffered from discrimination and prejudice. It was not until Martin Luther King led the fight for civil rights in the 1960s that black Americans became equal citizens.

Chapter 9 (The government of the USA) describes the three separate but equal parts of the government of the USA: the President, Congress, and the Supreme Court. The President is elected every four years and is the head of state. Congress makes the laws, but the President can refuse to approve them. The Supreme Court decides what the laws mean.

Chapter 10 (Living in the USA) talks about the USA as the richest country in the world. However, there are still many poor Americans. There is no state religion and there is freedom of speech for all.

Chapter 11 (Eating and drinking the American way) looks at 'Fast food', an American invention. Eating too many hamburgers, hot dogs, and french fries can lead to obesity. But across America you can eat the food of all nations.

Chapter 12 (Music from America) shows how American music has conquered the world. Jazz and blues are examples of black music. Country and western is the music of southern whites. Nowadays rap and hip-hop are popular with black and white youngsters alike.

Chapter 13 (Some great American cities) shows that whilst New York is the USA's biggest city, other American cities are important. Boston on the east coast is a centre of learning, while Los Angeles on the west coast is the centre of the film industry.

Chapter 14 (California) describes how California has the biggest population of any American state. It has high mountains and deserts. It also has the USA's most beautiful city, San Francisco.

Chapter 15 (Beautiful places to visit) shows how the USA has wilderness too. National Parks like Yosemite and Yellowstone protect nature and wildlife. And the Grand Canyon is one of the wonders of the world.

Chapter 16 (Hot and cold, big and small) describes the largest state in the USA - Alaska. Like Texas, it is now important for its oil. Hawaii and Florida attract people to live there because of their warm climates.

The USA
Pre-reading activity

What do you know?

1 What do you know about the USA? Tick the correct statements:

a New York is the capital of the USA. ☐
b Thirteen per cent of Americans are black. ☐
c The USA has borders with Canada and Mexico. ☐
d The US film industry is based in Sam Francisco. ☐
e Baseball is America's favourite sport. ☐
f The USA is made up of fifty states. ☐
g You can't drink alcohol in the USA until you're 21. ☐

2 How many of these Americans do you know? Match the people with the descriptions?

1 Martin Luther King	a first President of the United States
2 Walt Disney	b Native American woman who became friends with the first English settlers.
3 George Washington	c first black woman to be US Secretary of State for Foreign Affairs
4 Pocahontas	d black leader who led the fight for civil rights
5 Condoleezza Rice	e creator of Mickey Mouse

3 What do you think? Give your answers to these questions.

a Religion
There is no state religion in the USA and religion is not taught in schools. Why not? Do you think this is a good thing or a bad thing? Why?

b Equality
Slavery was abolished in 1867. But black Americans still suffer from prejudice. Why?

c Immigration
Millions of people left Europe for the USA in the late 19th and early 20th century. Why did they leave their homes? Why did the USA welcome them?

d Culture
Many ethnic groups want to keep their own traditions. They want to be Italian-Americans, Irish-Americans, Mexican-Americans. Is this a good thing? Are there any dangers in this attitude?

To the teacher

Aim: To prepare students to read about the story of the USA

Time: 20–30 minutes

Organization: 1 Use a map of the USA. Ask students to point out some features, e.g., the east coast and the west coast, New York, the Rockies (if shown). Or use an American flag: what do the stars stand for? (The number of US states now.) What do the stripes stand for? (The original thirteen American states.)Then ask them to do Exercise 1

either individually or in pairs.

Key 1: 1. Students should tick Statements b, c, e, f, and g. Students could flip through Chapter 1 to see if they can find the answers to any of the questions, e.g., b and f.

2. Ask students to see how many of these people they know. They shouldn't worry if they don't know many of these people. They will learn about them in the book.

Key 2: 3. 1d; 2 e; 3 a; 4 b; 5c.

Spot the mistakes

Read this summary of Chapter 7, New Americans, and correct the mistakes.

> *beginning*
> At the ~~end~~ of the 19th century America was mainly rural and there were many cities. But then farms were built and new cities grew up. America needed new workers. People from European countries like Ireland, Poland, and Mexico came to America. Often these immigrants were rich. Many had left because they had suffered from hunger, like the Irish, or from prejudice, like the Jews.
>
> America refused these newcomers. On the Statue of Liberty in New York harbour are the words: 'Give me your tired, your poor ...'
>
> Immigrants came from other countries too. More than 300,000 Japanese people came to live in California in the 19th century. Today most immigrants come from countries like Mexico and Puerto Rico and Italian has become America's second language.
>
> Although few immigrants want to learn English and become Americans, they also want to keep their own way of life. So in many cities there are areas called Chinatown or Little Italy. And on St Patrick's Day the whole of New York – not just the Italian-Americans – celebrates with a big party.

Now write a summary of the second part of Chapter 8, Black Americans, and include five mistakes. When you have written it, give it to someone to correct.

_____

_____

_____

To the teacher

Where: At the end of chapter 7

Aim: To consolidate comprehension of the importance of immigration as a factor in the growth of the USA

Time: 30 minutes

Key: The corrected summary should look like this:

At the *beginning* of the 19th century America was mainly rural and there were *few* cities. But then *factories* were built and new cities grew up. America needed new workers. People from European countries like Ireland, Poland, and *Italy* came to America. Often these immigrants were *poor*. Many had left because they had suffered from hunger, like the Irish, or from prejudice, like the Jews. America *welcomed* these newcomers. On the Statue of Liberty in New York harbour are the words: 'Give me your tired, your poor ...'

Immigrants came from other countries too. More than 300,000 *Chinese* people came to live in California in the 19th century. Today most immigrants come from Spanish-speaking countries like Mexico and *Spanish* has become America's second language.

Although *most* immigrants want to learn English and become Americans, they also want to keep their own way of life. So in many cities there are areas called Chinatown or Little Italy. And on St Patrick's Day the whole of New York – not just the *Irish-Americans* – celebrates with a big party.

The USA
After reading activity

Character crosswords

1 *Look at this crossword about President Reagan.*

```
FO R TIETH PRESIDENT
SPOK E WELL
WAS A N ACTOR
      G OVERNOR OF CALIFORNIA
BEC A ME PRESIDENT IN 1981
DIED I N 2004
```

2 *Make crosswords about these American presidents.*

.... K	.... L ....
.... E	.... I ....
.... N	.... N ....
.... N	.... C ....
.... E	.... O ....
.... D	.... L ....
.... Y	.... N ....

3 *Now choose one of these presidents and use the information in your crossword to write a short paragraph about him.*

_____

_____

_____

_____

_____

To the teacher

Aims: a) To recall key characteristics of important American presidents b) To write sentences from notes

Time: 30 minutes (Longer if internet is used.)

Organization: Ask students to work in pairs or small groups. Brainstorm key words that could be used in each crossword, e.g. KENNEDY might use killed, died, Dallas, young, elected; LINCOLN could use shot, slaves, North, born, etc.

You could ask students to research other presidents on the internet (using websites suggested in the in-book activities) and draw up crosswords for them.

Finally ask students to expand the 'crossword' notes so as to make full sentences and a short paragraph about one of the three presidents, e.g. Ronald Reagan was the fortieth President of the USA. He was an actor and he spoke well....

'Who, Sir? Me, Sir?'

K. M. Peyton

Introduction

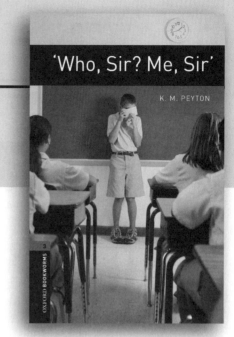

The story

Hawkwood School is just an ordinary school with ordinary pupils. Greycoats School, just along the road, is a rich school, for the children of rich parents.

One day, Sam Sylvester, one of the teachers from Hawkwood School, meets a Greycoats teacher. The two teachers agree to organize a tetrathlon competition between the two schools. In a tetrathlon, two teams of four compete in running, swimming, shooting and cross-country horse riding. Greycoats School has often competed in tetrathlon competitions, but for Hawkwood it is a new experience.

The four boys selected for the team are not very enthusiastic, but the captain, a girl called Nutty, encourages them and the first swimming lessons don't go too badly. The team also acquires its horses – four old horses that are saved from the knackers, where they would have been killed and turned into dog food. The horses are not in very good condition, and the boys realise that it is going to be a lot of work to look after them. Nails, the elder brother of one of the boys in the team, gets very interested in the horses and asks Nutty to help him learn to ride.

Then there is a shock. The riding lessons are going to be too expensive for the school. Sam Sylvester tells the team that the competition is dead.

Nutty refuses to accept this. She reforms the team with herself, Nails, and two of the four original team members – Hoomey, and a Sikh boy called Jazz. She arranges riding lessons, and Nails, who is a very good swimmer, takes on the swimming lessons. Some of the swimming takes place secretly in the private pool of the Smiths – while the Smiths are out for the evening. The Smiths' son is in the Greycoats team, but when Mr Smith finds out about the swimming he is so impressed that the Hawkwood pupils are organizing everything themselves that he allows them to continue – and also arranges shooting lessons for them.

The competition itself takes most of a day. At the beginning the Greycoats team get ahead – partly because they cheat by substituting a better swimmer in the swimming competition. Then the Hawkwood team

pull back – by cheating in the riding competition. When the competition finishes and it becomes apparent that both teams have cheated, there is only one thing to do – organize another competition next year. The teams are horrified.

Background to the story

The story has as a background the rivalry that inevitably exists between a private fee-paying school and a State comprehensive school. The Greycoats boys (as Mr Smith, one of their parents points out) have things organized for them, while the Hawkwood children not only have, in some cases, difficulties at home, but also have to fight a lot harder to get what they want. None of them are perfect, and Nails, in particular, is clearly a very difficult boy. The real star is Nutty, who is a born organizer, and who effectively pushes the boys in her team towards the result she wants.

Before reading

Here are some ways to help your students approach the story:

1 Give students the title of the book and show them the picture on the cover. Ask them to try and guess what kind of story it is.

2 Ask the students to read the text on the back cover of the book, and the story introduction on the first page. Then ask them a few questions about the story, or use the Before Reading Activities in the back of each Bookworm.

3 Use the pre-reading activity in this worksheet.

4 If there is a recording of this title, play the first few pages and stop at an interesting point.

'Who, Sir? Me, Sir?'

Pre-reading activity

Who's who?

1 *Match the words with the pictures.*

a Nutty and the others got on quickly and ran upstairs.

b Mr Potter had brought guns and targets with him.

c 'They can't kill poor old Bones!' Hoomey cried.

d Nails caught Hoomey by the chin and pulled his head out of the water.

e Bones wasn't going to stop until he won the race.

f 'Now come on, tell me what you want in life,' said Sam Sylvester.

g Mr Bean pushed the horse's rope into Hoomey's hand.

2 *Now write in the names of the people.*

a .... is an old horse.

b .... is a very bad swimmer, but he loves his horse ....

c .... is a policeman and an expert in shooting.

d .... is a good swimmer.

e .... is a teacher and Hoomey and Nutty are in his class.

f .... is a girl with big round glasses.

To the teacher

Aim: To familiarize the students with the setting and characters

Time: 10–15 minutes

Organization: Give one copy of the worksheet to each student or group of students. Ask them to match the words with the pictures. From the results of this matching activity they should be able to write in the names of the characters in Activity 2.

Key: Activity 1: 1f, 2d, 3g, 4c, 5a, 6b, 7e.

Activity 2: a Bones, b Hoomey, c Mr Potter, d Nails, e Sam Sylvester, f Nutty.

'Who, Sir? Me, Sir?'

While reading activity

Who thought it?

Who thought these words?

————— Chapter 1 —————

WHAT THEY THOUGHT	WHO THOUGHT IT
1 'They're rich but they're not better.'	
2 'I wish that I could see every match.'	
3 'It's a pity that Gloria's little sister is so stupid.'	
4 'I wish that we hadn't gone to that match with Mr Sylvester.'	

————— Chapter 2 —————

WHAT THEY THOUGHT	WHO THOUGHT IT
1 'I'd like to swim as well as Nails.'	
2 'I wish that I was back in the circus.'	
3 'I'm tired – and hungry.'	
4 'I'll help get the factory ready, but they can look after the horses.'	

————— Chapter 3 —————

WHAT THEY THOUGHT	WHO THOUGHT IT
1 'This is a lot better than home.'	
2 'I wonder why Nails wants to learn to ride.'	
3 'It was a good idea but we haven't got the money.'	
4 'Good. It was all too much hard work.'	

————— Chapter 4 —————

WHAT THEY THOUGHT	WHO THOUGHT IT
1 'If it's the only way to save the horses, I'll do it.'	
2 'It'll be quieter in here without those children.'	
3 'Are the Greycoats team better than us?'	
4 'Is Nutty's team better than us?'	

————— Chapter 5 —————

WHAT THEY THOUGHT	WHO THOUGHT IT
1 'Who was that in the pool?'	
2 'How are we going to get our clothes back?'	
3 'What are those children doing in the middle of town?'	
4 'I thought he was rich and horrible, but he's really rather nice.'	

————— Chapter 6 —————

WHAT THEY THOUGHT	WHO THOUGHT IT
1 'I must stay on! I don't want to die!'	
2 'Ah, music. I love dancing.'	
3 'What does he want at this time in the morning?'	
4 'I can think of a good way of cheating.'	

To the teacher

Where: At the end of each chapter
Aim: To revise the story development
Time: 5 minutes for each chapter

Organization: Give one copy of the worksheet to each student or group of students. Ask the students to decide who thought the words – tell the students that they will not find the words in the text.

'Who, Sir? Me, Sir?'

After reading activity

What happened to them?

At the end of the story the important characters are still young. Perhaps some of these things happened to them when they were older. Who do you think they happened to and why?

NAME	WHAT HAPPENEND?	COMMENTS
Nutty	. . . became a swimmer.	
	. . . went to prison.	
	. . . got a job working with animals.	
Jazz	. . . became a teacher.	
	. . . became Prime Minister.	
Nails	. . . married Seb and became very rich.	
	. . . was always poor.	
Hoomey	. . . was a competitor in the Olympic Games.	
	. . . was in the competition next year.	
	. . . became a policeman/woman.	
Sam Sylvester	. . . never rode a horse again.	
	. . . became a doctor.	

To the teacher

Aim: To think about the characters
Time: 10–20 minutes
Organization: Give one copy of the worksheet to each student or group of students. Ask them to think

which of these things might happen to each character in the future. They should then write down a new prediction for each of the five names.

The Wind in the Willows

Kenneth Grahame

Introduction

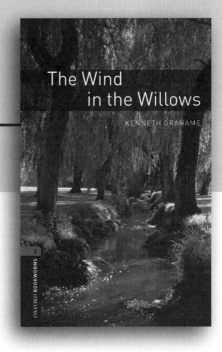

The story

The Wind in the Willows is a children's story about life on the river bank and the animals who live there. It's spring time and Mole decides to go for a walk. He eventually comes to the river where he meets Ratty the Water Rat. They go for a trip in Ratty's boat and have a picnic on the river bank and Mole and Ratty soon become good friends.

One day that summer, Ratty takes Mole to meet Toad. Toad is a very colourful character and is always trying something new. Last spring it was boating, this summer it is caravaning. The three friends go off together in Toad's caravan but when they are passed by a very fast motor car, Toad is transfixed. He now, wants to buy a car.

Mole has wanted to meet Badger for a long time and one day, sets off through the Wild Wood to visit him. But the Wild Wood is a frightening place and soon Mole gets lost and is very scared. Luckily, Ratty comes to look for him and they find Badger's house. They receive a very warm welcome and have dinner and stay the night.

The next summer Badger decides it is time to tell Toad to be more sensible as he is driving like a madman and always getting into trouble with the police. So one day he takes Ratty and Mole to Toad Hall to talk to Toad but Toad won't listen and runs away. He is soon caught by the police for stealing a car and put in prison. But he makes friends with the prisonkeeper's daughter who helps him escape disguised as a washerwoman. When he finally gets back to the river bank Ratty tells him the bad news that Toad Hall has been taken over by the Stoats, Weasels and Ferrets from the Wild Wood. However, Badger has a plan. He knows that there are secret tunnels from his house to Toad Hall which they can use to surprise the Wild Wooders in order to take back the Hall. Their plan is a success and after that, Toad promises to live quietly and be sensible.

Background to the story

The Wind in the Willows was not an immediate success with the public when it was first published. However, its popularity grew after it was dramatized as *Toad of Toad Hall* in 1929 by A A Milne, author of the *Winnie-the-Pooh* stories. It might have been this connection that resulted in the two authors using the same artist, E H Shepard, to illustrate their books. In the same way that Milne wrote his *Winnie-the-Pooh* stories for his only son Christopher Robin, *The Wind in the Willows* grew out of a series of letters and stories written by Grahame for his only son Alistair. Today, both these works have become part of the Canon of British Literature.

Before reading

Here are some ways to help your students approach the story:

1 Give students the title of the book and show them the picture on the cover. Ask them to try and guess what kind of story it is.

2 Ask the students to read the text on the back cover of the book, and the story introduction on the first page. Then ask them a few questions about the story, or use the Before Reading Activities in the back of each Bookworm.

3 Use the pre-reading activity in this worksheet.

4 If there is a recording of this title, play the first few pages and stop at an interesting point.

The Wind in the Willows

Pre-reading activity

Match the pictures with the chapter headings

CHAPTER HEADINGS

a   The river
b   The open road
c   The Wild Wood
d   A meeting with Mr Badger
e   A lesson for Mr Toad
f   Toad's adventures
g   Return to Toad Hall

To the teacher

Aim: To familiarize students with the story and its setting

Time: 15–20 minutes

Organization: Give one copy of the worksheet to each student, or to each group of students. Ask them to match the pictures with the correct chapter headings. When the students have done this, check the answers with them. Then ask them to write captions for each picture which you can compare and discuss afterwards. Finish by asking them to put the pictures in the order they might appear in the story and to predict in general terms what the story might be.

Key: 1e, 2g, 3a, 4f, 5d, 6b, 7c.

The Wind in the Willows
While reading activity

Who says what?

Read the character descriptions and write the name of the character in the box. Then read the quotes and match them to the descriptions. Write two more pieces of information that you can find about them in the lines provided.

a ....

Went on a picnic with
Ratty.
Isn't very brave.
Got lost in the Wild
Wood.

....

....

b ....

Lives on the river bank.
Is very good at rowing.
Owns a gun.

....

....

c ....

Is always trying something
new.
Is very lazy.
Has been in hospital
twice.

....

....

d ....

Lives in the Wild Wood.
Always knows what's
going on.
Doesn't like crowds.

....

....

e ....

Is very brave.
Knows all the paths in the
Wild Wood.
Is a good friend of Ratty's.

....

....

QUOTES

1 'There is nothing – really
nothing – nicer than just
messing about in boats ...'

2 'Afraid?' 'I don't think
any of them would argue
with me.'

3 'This is not the kind of
night for small animals to
be out.'

4 'I've finished with silly old
caravans for ever.'

5 'I'm so pleased to see
you!' I've been so
frightened, I can't tell
you!'

CHARACTERS
Badger
Toad
Otter
Mole
Rat

To the teacher

Where: At the end of Chapter 5
Aim: To revise the main characters
Time: 15–20 minutes
Organization: Give one copy of the worksheet to each student, or to each group of students. Ask them to identify the characters from their short descriptions and to write the correct name in the boxes. Then ask them to read the quotes and match them to the character descriptions. This can of course, be done at the same time if preferred. Then ask the students to look in their books and find two more pieces of information about the characters and write them in the spaces below. When they have finished, check and compare the answers with the rest of the class. Then get them to discuss the other animals mentioned in the story so far, and what kind of characteristics and personalities the author thinks they might have e.g. hedgehogs, weasels, stoats etc. This could be developed into a prediction activity where students guess future events in the story based upon the character descriptions they have discussed.
Key: 1b Rat, 2e Otter, 3d Badger, 4e Toad, 5a Mole.

The Wind in the Willows
After reading activity

Possible futures

It is ten years later. Read this section of a letter from Otter to Ratty and write a reply.

> I saw dear old Badger the other day. This new metro line through the Wild Wood means it's much easier to visit him than before. We had a lovely dinner in front of the fire and he told me all the news. He had just received an e-mail from Toad who misses us all of course, but he loves his new life in the city. Who would have thought he would become such a computer expert. This new system he's designed is a great success and he's always appearing on television or the radio. Apparently, he's got a flat in New York . . .
>
> What about you? Are you and Mole enjoying your holiday in the Lake District. I bet Mole is having a wonderful time doing lots of water skiing. He's become quite an expert these days. I passed by your old house yesterday Ratty and the new owner seems very friendly. Looking forward to seeing you after your holiday . . .

To the teacher

Where: At the end of the book
Aim: To revise characters and plot through imaginative re-writing
Time: 20–25 minutes
Organization: Give out one copy of the worksheet to each student, or to each group of students. Discuss the letter with the class and brainstorm some ideas and reactions before asking them to write a reply. In this way, it will encourage them to use their imagination and to see how far they can stretch the boundaries for new story lines. Encourage them to provide as much information as possible about the lives of the characters, the Wild Wood and recent and past events and to really use their imaginations. In doing this, the students have to reassess and refamiliarize themselves with characters and events in the story in order to develop them in their re-writing of the future. When the task is completed, students can then discuss and compare their letters.

Wyatt's Hurricane

Desmond Bagley

Introduction

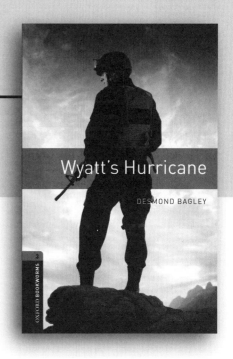

The story

The island of San Fernandez has not had a hurricane since 1910, but David Wyatt thinks that this is about to change. David Wyatt is a young West Indian weatherman researching hurricanes with the US navy. He feels 'Mabel' will hit San Fernandez soon and kill thousands of people and drown the capital St Pierre. As Wyatt has no proof, Schelling, his boss, will not warn the islanders.

But Causton, an English reporter with a London newspaper believes Wyatt's instinct. He also believes that Favel, a rebel leader, is planning war against the dictator, Serrurier. Everyone thinks Favel is dead but Causton, like Wyatt, can 'smell' trouble.

Both Wyatt and Causton are right, and there is a race to convince somebody to tell the islanders to move to higher ground while fighting rages around them. Captain Brooks at the U.S. base believes Wyatt, but cannot leave while there is a possibility of a civil war; Serrurier screams at Wyatt and Causton to leave him alone. Only Favel, the rebel leader, truly listens to Wyatt and orders his soldiers to move the people up the Negrito valley. Although a gentle and intelligent man, Favel thinks the hurricane is not just a disaster but an advantage in battle. He knows that once his troops leave St Pierre, Serrurier's men will move in and be killed by the hurricane. Wyatt, honest and idealistic, is disgusted by the reality of war but he is powerless to save everybody.

After escaping imprisonment, Wyatt leaves St Pierre with Causton and Favel's men. It is only when the 250-kilometre-hour winds have stopped, and the tidal waves have covered St Pierre, that Wyatt finds Julie, his fiancée. She is safe but injured by a falling tree.

Now Favel, the new president, must begin rebuilding the island. Captain Brooks offers help but it will be a long time before Mabel will be forgotten.

Background to the story

The fictional island of San Fernandez is located somewhere in the Caribbean, which is a hurricane area, and has suffered political unrest over the last fifty years. Both phenomena cause great misery and loss of life although arguably the second is preventable.

Hurricanes in this part of the world occur in early and late summer. They can cause damage directly by wind, pressure and rain and indirectly through storm surges and floods. Winds in excess of 185 kilometres an hour, and pressure of more than 400 kilograms per square metre can cause immense physical damage to buildings. Coastal waters can rise and the resulting sudden tide causes flooding in itself as well as preventing the normal outflow of rivers into the sea. Heavy rainfall can also lead to flooding and landslides. It is not surprising then that people in the path of a hurricane must seek shelter on higher ground and in the basements or ground floors of buildings in plenty of time in order to save their lives.

The urgency of evacuation and the terror invoked by a hurricane are both perfectly portrayed in the story. Even experienced war reporters like Causton and hurricane experts like Wyatt have the sense to fear the might of nature.

Before reading

Here are some ways to help your students approach the story:

1 Give students the title of the book and show them the picture on the cover. Ask them to try and guess what kind of story it is.

2 Ask the students to read the text on the back cover of the book, and the story introduction on the first page. Then ask them a few questions about the story, or use the Before Reading Activities in the back of each Bookworm.

3 Use the pre-reading activity in this worksheet.

4 If there is a recording of this title, play the first few pages and stop at an interesting point.

STAGE 3

Wyatt's Hurricane

Pre-reading activity

Name the book

Read the summary of the book you are going to read.

Hurricane Mabel is far out in the Atlantic Ocean and moving slowly northwards. Perhaps it will never come near land at all. But if it hits the island of San Fernandez, many thousands of people will die. There could be winds of more than 250 kilometres an hour. There could be a huge tidal wave from the sea, which will drown the capital city of St Pierre. Mabel will destroy houses, farms, roads, bridges . . .

Only one man, David Wyatt, believes that Mabel will hit San Fernandez, but nobody will listen to him . . .

Look at the chapter titles from the book and decide what you think is the best order. Together tell the story.

CHAPTER TITLES	ORDER
A night of fear	
Peace at last	
A night out in St Pierre	
Mabel hits the island	
The big wind is coming	
The battle for St Pierre	
Favel's plan	
Wyatt's warning	
The eye of the hurricane	
Flying into the hurricane	

Now choose the most suitable book title from below.

WYATT'S HURRICANE

The Battle for San Fernandez

THE EYE of THE STORM

THE BIG WIND

WYATT AND MABEL

To the teacher

Aim: To anticipate plot and theme
Time: 20 minutes
Organization: Give out the worksheet to pairs of students. Do not include the title of the book. Emphasize that the right answer is not important – students only have to justify their ideas and think creatively. Later, when the students have read the book, ask them to think back to this activity and decide whether they think that the title they chose is still the most suitable.

Wyatt's Hurricane

After reading activity

Hurricane board game

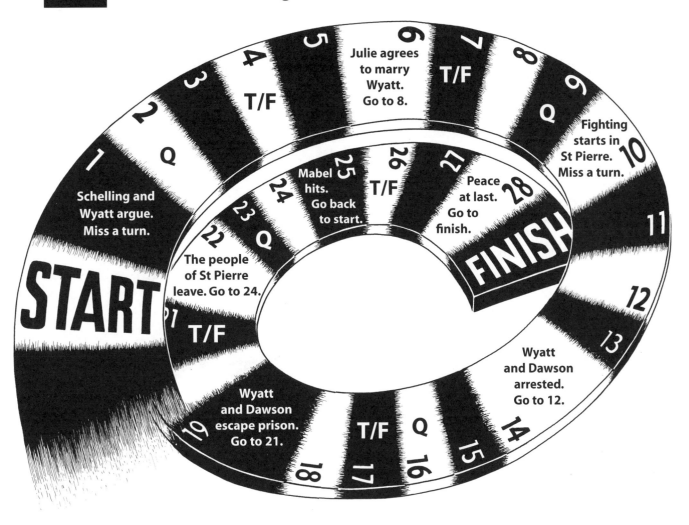

Rules

1 A dice is needed.
2 Whatever the dice says is the number of squares moved.
3 If you land on a blank there are no problems.

4 If you land on a T/F square, another player will ask you a True/False question from the T/F pack of cards. If you answer correctly you stay on the square. If you are wrong, you go back to your last square.

5 If you land on a Q, another player will take a Quotation card and ask you who the speaker is. Follow rule 4 for correct and wrong answers.
6 To win, a player must throw the exact number needed.

To the teacher

Aim: To revise plot and character
Time: 30 minutes
Organization: Divide the class into groups of between three and four students. Distribute a board and the two sets of cards to each group. Go through the rules and make sure everyone has understood them. Materials needed (per group of students):

1 board (on this page); 1 set of True/False cards; 1 set of Quotation cards; 1 dice; 1 small token or object for each student to move around the board (ask students to bring their own tokens, e.g. different coloured buttons). Numbers in brackets are page references.

QUOTATIONS

'If I have to fly through another storm like that, I'm going to take a ground job.' (4)

'Where there's a newsman, there's always trouble.' (10)

'Perhaps there will be another wind soon, too . . . Favel is coming down from the mountains.' (15)

'He believes that the Americans have paid for the rebels' guns – which of course is not true.' (19)

'We do not have hurricanes in San Fernandez. Get out!' (20)

'I think Wyatt can smell bad weather coming.' (23)

'Spies! Spies! American spies!' (24)

'I'm looking for a man called Wyatt.' (31)

'Brookes is afraid we'll take the Base if he leaves . . .' (32)

'If necessary, you'll have to shoot a few. There's no time to explain or to argue with them.' (35)

'But it's murder!' (36)

'War is murder.' (36)

'It's Dave. It must be. He's managed to warn the people of St Pierre about the hurricane. He's alive!' (41)

'This war will be over in ten minutes . . . No one can fight a war in a hurricane.' (43)

'You'll be a famous man because of your hurricane.' (48)

'What do you need most, Mr Favel, and where do you need it?' (52)

TRUE / FALSE

Wyatt is frightened of flying into the eye of a hurricane. (2)

Julie Marlow works for an American airline. (7)

Causton is an Englishman working for a big American newspaper. (7)

Wyatt had no real reason for thinking Mabel would hit San Fernandez. (6)

Wyatt warns Captain Brooks that Mabel will create a tidal wave that will destroy the U. S. base. (18)

Wyatt and Dawson go to Serrurier to warn him about the hurricane. (20)

Julie, Rawsthorne and Mrs Warmington escaped from St Pierre in Wyatt's car. (26)

Wyatt and Dawson are able to escape from prison because a bomb damaged the wall. (28)

Julie leaves Wyatt a message written in lipstick on the mirror of her hotel room. (30)

Manning doesn't believe there will be a hurricane until he sees the U. S. navy leave the base. (33)

Favel tells Manning to get the people out of St Pierre and up the Negrito valley. (35)

Favel is pleased that the hurricane will kill a few thousand of Serrurier's soldiers. (35)

Serrurier has 10,000 more soldiers than Favel. (37)

Julie, Rawsthorne and Mrs Warmington sheltered in a large hole above the Negrito valley. (41)

When the hurricane had stopped, St Pierre was under water. (46)

Wyatt is quietly pleased that Dawson wants to put him in one of his books. (48)